★ ★ ★ ★ ★ ★ ★ ★ ★

AMERICA'S
HORSES

★ ★ ★ ★ ★ ★ ★ ★ ★ ★ ★

AMERICA'S HORSES

A Celebration of the Horse Breeds Born in the U.S.A.

Moira C. Harris

Photographs by Bob Langrish

THE LYONS PRESS

GUILFORD, CONNECTICUT
An imprint of The Globe Pequot Press

For Elizabeth, who always found a way to
make horses happen in my life

Copyright © 2003 by Moira C. Harris
Photographs © Bob Langrish, with the exception of the following:
Photographs in the "American Cream Draft Horse" chapter © Dusty L. Perin/Lady-hawke Images
Photographs in the "Racking Horse" chapter © Sandra Hall

First Lyons Press paperback edition, 2006

The Lyons Press is an imprint of The Globe Pequot Press.

10 9 8 7 6 5 4 3 2 1

Printed in China

Text Design: M. A. Dubé

ISBN-13 : 978-1-59228-893-9
ISBN-10 : 1-59228 893 6

The Library of Congress has previously cataloged an earlier (hardcover) edition as follows:

Harris, Moira C.
America's horses : a celebration of the horse breeds born in the U.S.A. / Moira C. Harris ; Photographs by Bob Langrish.
p. cm.
ISBN 1-58574-822-6 (HC : alk. paper)
1. Horse breeds—United States. 2. Horse breeds—United States—Pictorial works. 3. Horses—United States. 4. Horses—United States—Pictorial works. I. Langrish, Bob. II. Title.
SF290.U6H37 2003
636.1'00973—dc 21
2003001797

CONTENTS

Preface vii

The Horse in North America ix

THE HORSES OF AMERICA

The American Cream Draft Horse 3

The American Paint Horse 9

The American Quarter Horse 19

The American Saddlebred 31

American White and
     American Creme 45

The Appaloosa 53

The Azteca 65

The Bashkir Curly 73

The Chincoteague Pony 79

The Colorado Ranger Horse 89

The Florida Cracker Horse 95

The Miniature Horse 101

The Missouri Fox Trotter 109

The Morab 117

The Morgan 123

The Mustang 135

The National Show Horse 147

The Palomino 157

Pony of the Americas 165

The Racking Horse 171

The Rocky Mountain Horse 175

The Standardbred 183

The Tennessee Walking Horse 191

Breed Associations 201

Index 207

PREFACE

SINCE THE BEGINNING OF RECORDED TIME, our history has been intertwined with that of the horse.

America's relationship with its horses goes beyond culture, language, society, and history. We have benefited from our multiple associations with equines, both at work and at play. It is a partnership built on the mutual understanding of each other's strengths and weaknesses—and one that has been a success. Whether toiling in the field, galloping down the backstretch, or bringing home that first blue ribbon, the animal that has inspired myth and legend is also flesh and bone—forever changing the lives that it touches.

The horse helped defend our country against our foes, carried us into battle against ourselves in the Civil War, took us to areas unknown, and made those territories home. We relied on his willingness, his endurance, and his strength; and the horse did not let us down.

America's economy depended almost entirely on horsepower up until the early part of the twentieth century. However, even today, in parts of America, you will still see the horse working in various capacities where modern equipment just can't cut it. From cattle ranches to Amish farms, the horse still plays a vital role in day-to-day operations.

Today, American horses embody our character as our partners in sporting events, from racing to international competition. They've given us wings to soar when we are decidedly earthbound. They still take us to new frontiers, making the journey just as pleasurable as the destination. Their kind nature makes them ideal to help the handicapped find their feet in a way that no mere machine can. Finally, American horses are good for the soul, because they allow us to take part in a connection, a partnership, which knows no words.

In this book, you will read about many different kinds of horses nurtured on American soil. While some share similar backgrounds, each was created to perform a certain role, a purpose, that has often changed upon the discovery of a new use for a breed's talents. From their history, to their conformation and characteristics, to what sports and specialties the horse excels in, *America's Horses* reveals the fascinating stories of this country's well-known and little-known breeds. Perhaps you'll even discover one so special that you'll be inspired to include that breed in your future.

THE HORSE IN NORTH AMERICA

MOST AMERICANS TRULY VALUE HORSES and all that they symbolize, yet many don't know how they came to be, or that the horse's first home was right on American soil. Although modern society seems light years away from the days when the horse was merely a beast of burden or ran wild on the plains, we still appreciate the role they have played in the past. We also look forward to a future where they continue to enrich our lives.

The Dawn Horse

Eohippus, the precursor to the modern horse, had more in common with a tiny deer than it did with Secretariat. It existed approximately fifty million years ago, and was about the size of a fox, with a rounded back and short neck. It had three toes on its little hind feet and four on the front. Small enough to conceal itself in the brush that it survived on, this prey animal preferred the technique of camouflage rather than that of flight. This Dawn Horse, as *Eohippus* is often called, was a browser of leaves, not a grazer of grass.

As the centuries passed, the little deerlike horse evolved. As its environment changed, so it too adapted. When grasslands formed in North America, its ancestral home, the animal developed larger teeth with which to crop grass. Its legs grew longer and the bone more dense, to support a heavier frame. It originally traveled on all its toes, but through evolution, the side toes, no longer used, began to recede, and *Eohippus* walked mostly on its middle toe. Thousands of years passed, and the animal's shape gradually changed to reflect its surroundings. No longer did it require a hunched-over body. Through natural selection, the horse began to travel more quickly, fleeing predators instead of merely hiding from them. *Mesohippus* and *Miohippus* were the successors of the Dawn Horse, existing about twenty-five to forty million years ago. The first single-hoofed horse, *Pliohippus,* emerged approximately six million years ago. Half a million years before man, and about a million years ago, the side toes receded completely, and an animal with strong teeth and jaws, a long sloping neck, sturdy back, strong hooves, and legs suitable for running materialized. This animal was known as *Equus,* and is the species we know today as the horse.

However, the horse that was the precursor to every modern horse breed was not exactly the picture of what we see today. A million years ago, *Equus* was still very primitive looking, probably sporting a wild, thick coat, bushy mane and tail, dark stripes on the legs, and a stripe along the spine.

About fifteen thousand years ago, humans arrived in the Americas. At about the same time, the horse began to disappear from its birthplace, for reasons that remain a bit of a mystery. The human population may have decimated the equine population to the point where it couldn't recover. Climatic changes after the end of the last Ice Age also could have been a major factor. Whatever occurred, the horse was thriving in Eurasia and Africa, having migrated over an ancient land bridge that was now below sea level. Wild equine species did very well in this part of the world, and their numbers increased by the thousands. Five thousand years later, horse met human in the Ukraine, and the tribes caught and tamed these horses, bringing about the first domesticated *Equus.*

But the horse in North America? It died out completely about ten thousand years ago. The equine presence in America was not felt again until Conquistadors arrived in the late fifteenth century with their ships, their weapons, and their robust, noble steeds.

From there, it was only a matter of time before American ingenuity, coupled with necessity, took over. Horses served as transportation, as colleagues in work, sporting partners, and friends to be cherished. Horses meant freedom—to explore, to take chances, to risk the unknown. Although horses today are used mainly for pleasure and not labor, their importance has only shifted, not diminished. America was built from the back of a horse.

THE HORSES
OF AMERICA

⋆ ⋆ ⋆ ⋆ ⋆ ⋆ ⋆ ⋆ ⋆ ⋆

THE AMERICAN CREAM DRAFT HORSE

THERE ARE WORKHORSES, and then there are workhorses. Drafts, the cold-blooded mammoths of the horse world, are known for having incredible strength paired with a docile temperament. Most draft breeds hail from Europe; only one, the American Cream Draft, originated in the United States. This is America's biggest workhorse.

Breed History

The breed sprang from a large, cold-blood-type mare with a rich, milky-yellow coat, a white mane and tail, pink skin, and amber-colored eyes. Sold at a livestock and farm auction in 1911 in Story County, Iowa, to a horse dealer named Harry (Hat) Lakin, she later became the first registered American Cream. Lakin used her in his breeding program and was delighted to see her produce the same light-colored foals for him, all of which sold handsomely. As years turned into decades and the mare's produce begat their own, it was clear that "Old Granny," as she became known, would be the originator of horses that distinctly and consistently resembled her in color and type.

A few colts of Old Granny's—including Buck No. 4 and Yancy No. 3—went on to sire more cream horses. However, the first and most noted stallion of the breed was Silver Lace, born in 1931. This horse covered mares over a large territory in central Iowa, and a majority of today's registered Creams are his direct descendants.

In the 1940s, the breed's major support came from C. T. Rierson of Hardin County, Iowa. Searching high and low, he bought up any available colts sired by Silver Lace and started building up his own herd. With the help of the horses' previous owners, he painstakingly recorded the pedigree of each. In 1944, Rierson wrote, "They are making a class for them at the... fair this year. This is the county

The amber eyes of the American Cream Draft Horse reflect its gentle, willing nature

in which they originated, and it will be the first time they have been shown in a class by themselves." The first officers of the American Cream Horse Association organized in March 1944, with Rierson as president.

In 1948, the National Stallion Enrollment Board recommended the breed be made official. Two years later, the Iowa Department of Agriculture recognized their breed standard. Rierson wrote in the official American Cream Horse pamphlet, "History is still in the making—our efforts are in the line of improvement. Our aim is to have the American Creams rated among the top draft breeds of America."

Seven years later, however, Rierson died and his herd of American Creams were sold and scattered across the region. By that time, 58 owners had registered 199 Creams in seven states, but the age of mechanization and the unwieldy size of modern farms spelled disaster for the young breed. In the years that followed, there

The American Cream may be a very light milky color, or may be much richer, but the skin underneath the beautiful coat will be pink.

COMPARABLE BREED

The Belgian, or Brabant, which often weighs more than a ton, has tremendous size and strength and has been in demand by European farmers for centuries. The American version of the Belgian is lighter, more refined, and bears a light chestnut coat with flaxen mane and tail.

was simply no use for draft horses, and a good number of them were, tragically, shipped off to slaughter to be made into pet food.

Not all were destroyed, however. Despite the Depression and World War II's effect on America's economy and farming, devout breeders clung to the stock they had left and continued to use them for farm work. Thanks to their efforts, which included using linebreeding, the American Cream Draft did not disappear. While its numbers were still dangerously low through the mid to late twentieth century, it still had enough support to keep afloat—and in 1982, the studbooks were reopened to uphold the original standards.

The American Minor Breeds Conservancy, aware of the delicate nature of the breed's future, placed the American Cream Draft on the list of "endangered" breeds. In 1990, Dr. E. Gus Cothran of the University of Kentucky was doing some research in blood typing. In a study he was conducting, he wanted to compare Creams to a variety of other breeds. By contacting owners and obtaining blood samples, he discovered that Creams were indeed a distinct breed of horse among drafts. He wrote, "The Creams are no more similar to the Belgian than they are to Suffolks, Percherons, or Haflingers." This study helped prove that Creams were not just a horse of a different color—they were a different horse altogether.

The more Cream breeding in the foal's background, the more certain that it too would turn out to have the same ivory color. In recent years, both inbreeding and linebreeding have helped produce a sustainable number of true Creams in both type and color. Currently, about 250 registered American Cream Draft Horses can be found around the globe.

*B*ecause of their rarity, an American Cream Draft is an extra special addition to a stable or ranch.

Breed Characteristics

The ideal American Cream, according to the 1948 American Cream pamphlet, is of course, a cream color—which may be light or rich colored, but must have pink, not gray or dark, skin. This factor is so important that American Cream breeders designate pink skin as the second most important characteristic after the cream coat. White markings, such as blazes and stockings, are sought after. Dark-skinned Creams often do not have acceptable color. Further, when mated with other Creams, a dark-skinned Cream generally produces foals that are too light or nearly white. The best color is actually achieved by mating two light-skinned Creams. Therefore, the most desirable American Creams have pink skin, correct color, and the white markings that contrast so beautifully with their coats.

Unlike true American White horses, Creams feature eyes that are the color of amber, or even a reddish brown. Foals are usually born with eyes so light they are nearly white, but which darken over time to a topaz color at maturity.

The American Cream Draft has a medium draft horse build, standing 15.1 to 16.3 hands high. Originally, they were more compact, weighing less than 1,400 pounds, but today's Cream tips the scales at more than 1,600 pounds. They have well-proportioned heads with straight profiles, arched necks and muscular bodies. They have nice activity at all gaits, which gives a finely matched team extra panache. The breed has represented itself in parades, including the illustrious Tournament of Roses Parade in Pasadena, California. A matched pair makes a stunning entrance to an elegant affair, and are occasionally used for weddings. American Cream Drafts are small enough to ride under saddle as well. They make excellent pleasure-riding mounts, and are sometimes seen in historical reenactments. Creams have no problem participating in open draft horse shows, however. Most are found on small Midwestern farms where they work to earn their keep, pulling plows, raking hay, and more.

Fans of the breed comment on how willing their Creams are, and how easygoing their nature is. The person who keeps a team wants one that is not only trustworthy, but also easy to train.

Probably the most famous of all American Cream Draft Horses are those that live and work as a team at Colonial Williamsburg, a popular historic eighteenth-century resort village in Virginia. Used for wagon and carriage rides, they were chosen for their rarity, as well as for the fact that they are members of the only American draft breed. Their use in Williamsburg not only lets the public in on this well-kept secret, but also allows their numbers to increase through the breeding program located there.

So if you notice a statuesque horse with topaz eyes and a coat the color of a tropical beach, you may unknowingly be gazing upon a rare find. Cherish your meeting with the American Cream Draft Horse; although it's uncommon, it is undoubtedly a massive equine treasure.

THE AMERICAN PAINT HORSE

"RIDE A PAINTED PONY, let the spinning wheel spin."

Who hasn't dreamed of slipping on the back of a horse splashed in color and white patches? To see a blue eye, often paired with a brown, peeking out from a thick thatch of forelock? Paints are beautiful creatures, and it's horses like these that epitomize our Western heritage. A horse marked with color running the gamut from subtle to outrageous has become synonymous with cowboys and Indians, cattle drives, wild horse roundups, and wide open spaces.

Breed History

To find the origins of the Paint, you'll have to head back in time several centuries. There is evidence of painted horses in ancient times, as seen in the art of past civilizations from Egypt and China to the Mediterranean. It seems that colorful horses splashed with white were quite popular in some parts of the world. One country, Spain, had a big influence on the future of the breed, with breeders selecting fine Oriental spotted horses to cross with native stock, resulting in foals bearing overo- and tobiano-patterned coats.

Early Spanish explorers made a host of voyages to the New World on behalf of their mother country. In 1519, Hernando Cortes's men landed on the shores of Mexico, and native people watched as horses were unloaded on land—the first equines in America since prehistoric times. Among their stock were loudly colored horses—pintos, as they were known, meaning "painted" in Spanish. The natives instantly gravitated to them and soon learned how horses could change their lives. Some bought horses from the Spanish settlements, while others stole them. Quickly

Even from dam to filly, no two colorful coats are exactly alike.

and skillfully developing their horsemanship, Native Americans found that the horse was not only an excellent beast of burden and transportation, he was also a partner in battle. Of all the horses in the natives' care, the horse that became prized among several tribes was the horse with splashy markings.

Painted horses migrated up into North America as well, and from Colonial times onward, these horses of Spanish ancestry were working on cattle ranches and American farms.

But not all spotted horses are necessarily American Paint Horses. Their story continues and becomes intermixed with that of the American Quarter Horse. In the 1690s, American colonists began crossing imported English horses with the Chickasaw Pony—which had originated in the Southeast from Spanish and Barb stock. The result was a small, hardy, and quick animal that was a willing work-horse during the week and a competitive match racehorse on the weekends.

This animal, which came to be known as the Quarter Running Horse, gained a reputation far and wide as the fastest horse over short distances. But more than that, it found another calling in the 1800s, when pioneers heading west needed hardy, willing horses to haul their wagons and carry cattlemen in the saddle. Toward the turn of the twentieth century, when ranching had spread country-wide, the Quarter Horse was legendary for its uncanny "cow sense."

In 1940, a group of horsemen came together to preserve the Quarter Horse breed and founded the American Quarter Horse Association (AQHA). They infused the breed with Thoroughbred blood, and then closed the stud book in 1962. The breed standard was very strict, especially when it came to color. Occasionally a foal of Quarter Horse parentage would be born with patches or splashes of white across its body. These horses were not embraced for their originality, but shunned. Many of these beautiful foals were culled by breeders—considered unfit to carry on the Quarter Horse name.

However, there were many horsemen and women who thought these pinto Quarter Horses were indeed beautiful—plus, they had the willing nature and

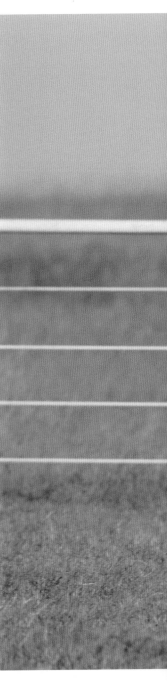

The tovero combines characteristics of both Paint horse patterns, with chest and flank spots varying in size. While the tovero's spots may look much like the tobiano's, the horse often will have the overo bald face.

hardiness that were so coveted by Quarter enthusiasts. To find a new home for these "outcroppings," two organizations formed, then joined together to become the American Paint Horse Association (APHA), a registry that helps preserve and promote the painted horse of Quarter Horse breeding. And so, since the early 1960s, the American Paint has taken a strong hold on western riders' affections. They love the flashy markings that come along with the even temperament and the willing nature. And like fingerprints, no two Paints bear the same markings, making this a versatile, head-turning horse.

Breed Characteristics

Paint Horses come in a variety of colors but they drape across the horse in two main patterns: tobiano and overo.

If you see a Paint, it's probably a tobiano, the most common pattern. A tobiano horse looks like a white horse with large, regular splashes of color across its body, often looking as though these colorful patches originate from its head (which

An overo's white seldom crosses over the back, and the horse often sports a good deal of white on its face. The lacy edge around the spots is also characteristic.

COMPARABLE BREED

While pinto horses exist in many different breeds, the Tinker Horse, known under a variety of other names (according to subtle type differences) such as Tinker Cob, Irish Gypsy Cob, and Vanner, hails from the UK and Ireland. These horses are distinguished by their gorgeous spotted coats, their Shire or Clydesdale conformation, and their ample feathering below the knee.

resembles that of a solid-colored horse), chest, flanks, and haunches. The white usually crosses over the top of the horse, and it often sports white legs as well. It may have a two-toned mane and tail.

In comparison, the overo paint looks like a colored horse sporting white, jagged markings that appear to have sprung from the horse's sides or belly. These splashes often appear as if they are paint spreading to the neck, tail, legs, and back. Overos often have white legs, but instead of having dark faces, they commonly have bald or all white faces. While tobianos have crisp, clean edges around their markings, overos' spots look as though they are framed in lace.

There is one more basic coat pattern of the American Paint Horse—the tovero, which combines the best of both overo and tobiano coloring. It carries the bald face of the overo, but sports the clean-edged spots of the tobiano. These horses are mostly white, but have dark coloring at the top of the head and around the muzzle, with smaller colored patches originating from chest and flank, with occasional spots around the tail.

How do you mix Paint to create those fine colorful specimens today? It doesn't happen with every single breeding, but to increase the likelihood of seeing spots on a foal's birthday, crossing two registered Paint horses is the most common method. But the APHA also allows Quarter Horses and Thoroughbreds into their registry—as long as they meet certain criteria. All horses that are accepted into the registry must be at least 14 hands high at two years of age.

Stallions must be inspected by the age of two years by an APHA representative, and must meet their standard. Of course, there is also the matter of spots. While some horses are loudly splattered with color, others may have only nominal markings. In this case, the rules govern that a horse has to have minimum "natural paint markings" more than two inches in diameter for regular registration, as well as one of several different characteristics. These include white leg markings that extend above the knees and/or hocks; a blue eye; an apron or bald face; white on the jaw or lower lip; a blue zone around the marking (where there appears to be a bluish outline around the marking); a two-tone mane, one color being natural white; dark spots or freckles in white hair on the face or legs; white areas completely surrounded by a contrasting color in the non-visible zone (the area that is not visible when looking at the horse in profile or head-on, excluding the head).

If a foal of Paint ancestry doesn't have enough color and characteristics to meet the regular registration, it is considered breeding stock—which means that the horse can still possibly produce a splashy foal when it grows up. But it won't be able to compete in APHA shows against its spotted relatives.

Paints in Action

Depending upon which genes they've inherited, Paint horses can do a variety of things under saddle, or in harness. Although originally popular among western riding enthusiasts, Paints are now being seen in the show-jumping arena, the dressage ring, and even under English saddle in hunter classes. For horses of Thoroughbred ancestry, these fleet-footed, colorful creatures can compete in Paint horse racing. However, the horse's true calling is as a stock horse, and you'll find Paints excelling in pleasure, trail, halter, and showmanship classes, and in reining, cutting, and roping, too.

You'll see all this and more at the American Paint Horse Association's World Show, held every June into July at the Will Rogers Memorial Center in Fort Worth, Texas. Big paybacks, two solid weeks of activities, and a schedule packed with events suited to every exhibitor's interests highlight the World

The American Paint Horse is renowned for its cow sense, making it an excellent choice for events like team roping.

The tobiano coat pattern has the dark color covering the flanks, while the legs are usually white. The spots are regular and have a distinct crisp edge, and the mane and tail can often be two-toned.

Championship Paint Horse Show. Each year, equestrians from nearly every state and several Canadian provinces participate.

To ensure the best possible judging at the World Show, APHA calls on specialty judges for certain classes. For reining, National Reining Horse Association (NRHA) judges will be used. National Cutting Horse Association (NCHA) judges will evaluate cutting horse competition. USA Equestrian (USAEq) judges will be called on for hunt-seat classes.

Those who are looking to put some Paint in their lives can find high-quality Paint horses for sale in conjunction with the World Show. Additionally, shoppers enjoy the Colors of the West trade show.

The best thing about the show is that it's an opportunity to see the spotted horse in action, where it's sure to change the way folks think about this colorful breed.

When watching high-quality Paint horses run, jump, spin, and trot, it's easy to understand why it's one of America's fastest growing breeds.

Famous Paints

For years **Yellow Mount,** born in 1964, was considered the epitome of what a Paint should be, both in conformation and performance. He was the first horse to be designated as Champion of the APHA, and was named the first Running Supreme Champion. He stood National Champion eight times, was a Superior Halter Horse, and earned Register of Merit awards in racing, western pleasure, calf roping, reining and barrel racing. Of the thirty-nine horses who have earned the title of APHA Supreme Champion, one is Yellow Mount and four are his progeny. He was also the first Paint horse to be cast as a Breyer model horse.

Adios Amigos was a famous reining champion and also made his name as a sire of many champion performance and halter horses. He was named National Champion Two-Year-Old Stallion in 1964. The following year, he won Reserve National Champion Three-Year-Old Stallion, and also won the reining championship, earning the highest score ever on a Paint reining score card—a record that stood for several years.

Heza Night Train, a Yellow Mount grandson, is known as Mr. Ed-iquette and, following his solid show career, he became a noted trick horse with more than fifty tricks learned. He entertained audiences of thousands at fairs, festivals, expos, parades, and in TV commercials. A model of him was cast by the Peter Stone Company.

Wahoo King, a loudly colored sorrel American Paint Horse, was one of the greatest calf roping horses, not just in his own breed, but of any breed. During the 1960s, he set the standard for others to beat with his partner Junior Robertson. They became widely known on the pro rodeo circuit in the days when it wasn't fashionable to be riding a spotted horse.

Rain, the animated costar of the DreamWorks film *Spirit: Stallion of the Cimarron,* became an official American Paint Horse when the APHA chose to honor her by awarding her an honorary registration certificate in recognition of the widespread exposure her producers gave the Paint Horse in the film. Rain is the first animated horse to receive such a nomination.

THE AMERICAN QUARTER HORSE

WHAT DO YOU DO IF YOU ARE THE most popular horse on the planet? Well, as every owner, rider, and admirer of the American Quarter Horse knows, the answer is just about anything. From reining to racing, from dressage to driving, the American Quarter Horse is the epitome of American ingenuity and versatility.

The American Quarter Horse is a national icon—just like mom, apple pie, hot dogs, baseball and pickup trucks. With each passing year, the Quarter Horse becomes more of an emissary for its country of origin. Capable of churning down the racetrack, soaring over a high puissance wall, crouching eye to eye with an errant calf, or elegantly displaying tempi changes of lead in a dressage test, the American Quarter Horse has fans in every riding discipline, and at every performance event.

That versatility has played a part in making the Quarter Horse the most popular and populous breed in the world, with more than four million horses registered. Another pleasing trait of the breed is its legendary temperament—it can do it all because of its need to please. Often described as level-headed, kind-hearted, and obedient, the Quarter Horse is many people's choice for their first mount. But this even temper doesn't mean that the Quarter Horse lacks a competitive spirit. In fact, Quarters have been successful in nearly every competitive arena.

The Quarter Horse's colorful history is entwined with our own, from Colonial times to frontier exploration. Like the country it hails from, it is diverse; the breed's many specialized bloodlines are capable of competing at the top of all equine endeavors. It's also adaptable, with countless horses going from show competitor, to family mount, to trail deputy in the off season.

Even at an early age, the American Quarter Horse's strength and stamina are evident.

Breed History

Spanish explorers brought their horses—Iberian stock with roots primarily in Oriental blood, such as Arabians, Barbs, and Turkmen horses—along in their exploration in the Americas. These horses were quite different from the colonists' horses that arrived later—English Thoroughbreds and English harness horses.

These Spanish horses were traded to or stolen by Native Americans; some escaped and went on to become the foundation of the Mustang. Florida's Chickasaw tribe took the Spanish stock and created their own distinct stock breed that became quite popular due to its lightning speed and quickness. Often called the Chickasaw Pony (or later, the Cracker Horse), they were usually under 14 hands high, close-coupled, and well muscled. They were fast over very short distances—sprinters to the core.

In the Colonies, breeders wanted to create a horse to be a willing partner in harness and under saddle during the work week, then be able to run in weekend races, as well as riding for pleasure. The colonists took great pride in having a horse at home that could sprint about a quarter mile, a popular sport at the time. So in typical American style, colonial breeders in Virginia, North Carolina, and South Carolina soon began blending various bloodlines in order to create a horse that would be able to do it all. They bred Chickasaws to their Thoroughbreds, English Pacers, and even some French stock. The Chickasaw horses proved to be the ticket to ride—and race. They gave the colonial horses the sprinting speed that was so coveted. With consistent breeding, a new type of horse came forth.

Of the Thoroughbred stallions used in breeding from 1746 to 1800, one stood out above the rest. His name was Janus, and he was directly related to one of the three founding oriental horses in the Thoroughbred breed. A great-grandson of the Godolphin Barb, Janus was not like the slender, long-legged

With lightning-fast breaks out of the starting gate, the American Quarter Horse is the fastest sprinting horse in the world.

Thoroughbred studs from England. He was well muscled and close-coupled, and breeders hoped that he'd pass these traits along to his offspring. To say he did is an understatement. Janus's foals were stocky and powerful—simply put, built for speed. Every foal seemed to carry the traits of ruggedness, strength, and athletic ability. Janus's services were in great demand, especially after his foals were old enough to be put to saddle and race. His blood coursed through the veins of what was now being called the American Celebrated Running Quarter Horse, the fastest breed for a quarter of a mile. Janus put his stamp on the breed, and even several generations later, his impact on the breed's conformation was indisputable. His place is sealed in history; all but two of the original eleven foundation lines trace back to him.

But racing was not all the celebrated horse could do. Because of his willing nature and solid work ethic, the Quarter Horse became sought after as an all-around partner. There was nothing the Quarter Horse couldn't do, it seemed, and even better, there was nothing the Quarter Horse would refuse to do.

When races were increased to additional furlongs, the Quarter Horse, with its shorter sprints, fell out of favor, and the Thoroughbred took the racing spotlight. Proper racecourses were built, and instead of match races held in fields and along country roads, distance races became the norm. This shift didn't diminish the demand for the Quarter Horse, however. It merely meant that the versatile breed took on a new challenge. That calling was heard from the West.

In the early 1800s, pioneers headed west to new claims. Some were looking for gold, others to escape the cities. The Quarter Horse was the chief mode of transportation, and settlers hitched up their wagons, taking their compact horses with them. The breed again proved itself worthy. It helped clear pastureland, plowed fields, hauled logs, and herded cattle. This was the horse's true destiny.

Settlers became ranchers, obtaining huge parcels of land—sometimes thousands of acres with countless head of cattle. What the ranchers didn't know was that the blood coursing in their little horses' veins was some of the most cow-savvy in the world. These horses had the innate ability to "read" a cow—to understand its body language. They had to be quick on their feet and go after a stray heifer or calf instinctively.

As the twentieth century began, all horses' fates were sealed with the first Model T that rolled off the assembly line. Mechanization could have spelled the end of all horse breeding, but once again, the Quarter Horse had a calling to answer—that of a companion horse. A group formed in 1940 to preserve and protect this American treasure. The American Quarter Horse Association not only made the horse's breed name official, but also established a studbook and developed bylaws for breeding.

Having helped settle the West of yesteryear, the American Quarter Horse has since become the most popular breed on the planet.

The first horse to be entered in that book was Wimpy, a misnomer if there ever was one. This deep chestnut stallion was stocky and powerfully built—so perfect, he was awarded the Grand Champion Stallion title by the AQHA in 1941.

The AQHA had incredible foresight. Seeking to promote the breed and increase its popularity, the AQHA touted its horse as a horse for all reasons: a ranch horse, a performance horse, a pleasure horse and, yes, still a racehorse. And Americans liked what they saw. Breeders refined bloodlines, so that not only was there a Quarter Horse that could do it all; there was also one breed that would be at the top of nearly all events.

The conformation of the American Quarter Horse is all about power, with its muscular hindquarters, close-coupled frame, level topline, and brawny forehand.

Breed Characteristics

Even with selective breeding for specialized events, it's not hard to spot a Quarter Horse in a crowd. Most are between 14.2 to 15.3 hands high, and weigh anywhere from 1,000 to 1,200 pounds. Their powerful muscling is evident under their burnished solid coats, especially in their hindquarters and shoulders.

The horse has a compact head with wide-set eyes, small, alert ears, delicate muzzle, and large nostrils to enhance breathing capacity. The jaws are trademark on some bloodlines: many sport large, powerful-looking cheekbones that have earned them the name "bulldog".

Quarter Horses have compact frames, sloping shoulders, deep barrels, broad chests, and clean legs. But the hindquarters—the Quarter Horse's powerplant—are what make this horse legendary. They are broad, well muscled and heavy, enabling the horse to propel itself forward without hesitation.

The AQHA recognizes thirteen color variations in the breed, including bay, gray, palomino, red roan, blue roan, buckskin, grulla, and black. However, the most common coat color you'll find in the breed is sorrel, a burnished chestnut. Quarter Horses can have some white markings on the face, such as a blaze, star, snip, or strip, and can have white below the knees, such as stockings or socks. But if the horse has too much white—for instance, big splashes of white on the body, a large bald face, or white above the knees—it's considered a crop-out. Crop-outs are what started the American Paint Horse breed, so they can be registered with the APHA, or they can be gelded or spayed and registered with the AQHA under a hardship clause.

Today's Quarter Horse is different from those of even two decades ago. Although outcrossing with other breeds stopped with the closing of the studbook in 1962, Thoroughbred blood is still allowed into the breed in the form of the Appendix registry. Appendix horses are the result of breeding either a Thoroughbred with an American Quarter Horse; or breeding an Appendix American Quarter Horse with a registered American Quarter Horse.

Appendix horses are given papers on different color stock and have the letter X in front of their registration number, so it is easily recognizable that the horse has Thoroughbred blood. An Appendix horse can gain regular status in the numbered catalog by obtaining a Register of Merit—a record of outstanding performance. To receive this, a horse must acquire ten points in the difficult open AQHA performance classes or on the racetrack. Once the Appendix horse shows his worthiness, his papers go from gold to white, and the X is removed from his number. And so the Thoroughbred/Quarter Horse blend becomes considered full Quarter Horse, and the breed continues to be infused with Thoroughbred blood.

While today's Quarter Horse is still powerful and compact, the influx of Thoroughbred bloodlines, as well as the demand for lighter horses in the western rail classes, has made the horse more refined, taller, lankier—in essence, more like a Thoroughbred. This doesn't bother many enthusiasts, who argue that the breed originated with Thoroughbreds, so there is no reason not to continue breeding to them. However, others long for the bulldog type, the foundation, old-style horse that was small, compact, upright, and rippling with bulging muscles. Groups formed to preserve this branch of the Quarter Horse family, too, so future generations will never miss out on the past.

COMPARABLE BREED

The Australian Stock Horse. An amalgamation of Thoroughbred, Arabian, European, and South African horses, this breed was sought after as a cavalry mount because of its strength and endurance. Its conformation is similar to that of the American Quarter Horse, with a well-proportioned, well-muscled frame, clean legs, and strong hooves. It also has a similar kind temperament and willingness.

And it is the past that allows people to learn from mistakes and correct them. For instance, breeders only a short time ago sought to produce large-boned Quarters with small hooves. While some felt that these "teacup" feet were attractive, they were fraught with problems, the most prominent one being navicular disease. Most breeders, after becoming aware of the lameness issues that befall a small-hoofed horse, bred that trait out.

Another hard lesson for some to learn was illustrated when champion halter horse Impressive developed hyperkalemic periodic paralysis, an inherited muscle disorder that makes muscle cells unable to manage electrical impulses effectively. The result was muscle weakness and "attacks"—episodes of tremors that could last for a few minutes or a few hours, and could be mild to severe, with the most extreme instances causing death from cardiac arrest or respiratory failure. Horses that carried the HYPP disorder—even though they showed no symptoms—could pass it along to their offspring. Many breeders who bred for big prizes without regard for the horse continued to produce specimens with this dreadful condition. Fortunately, the AQHA stepped in and discouraged breeders from offering the stud services of HYPP-positive horses.

Today, no other horse can rival the Quarter Horse's sheer numbers. The American Quarter Horse Association's World Show, held every October in Oklahoma City, is testament to the true versatility of the breed. One showcase event is the crowning of the Superhorse, the horse earning the most points in at least three separate disciplines over the course of the show. Perhaps the most famous Superhorse was Rugged Lark, who won the title in both 1985 and 1987, ridden by Lynn Palm. It seemed Lark could do everything, without effort, from dressage and hunter classes, to western events. To add to his crown, Rugged Lark is the only Superhorse to have sired two other Superhorse winners: The Lark Ascending in 1991 and Look Who's Larkin' in 1999.

At the World Show everything is top notch. Most breed associations only dream of what the AQHA can do. Not only does the show draw the finest Quarter Horse flesh in the world, it beckons the best riders, trainers, grooms, and vendors to show their stuff. Competitors are known to have a different outfit for each class they ride in. Trainers are paid thousands of dollars for their services during the

While most American Quarter Horses are known for being savvy around cattle, many also excel in the hunter and jumper world.

two-week show. Grooms burn the midnight oil so each of their charges is impeccable under the lights of the indoor show pen. Vendors, from tack shops to trailer manufacturers, show their wares to a very enthusiastic shopping public.

And the horses? Well, they're the best of the best. All around. Versatile. Athletic. As American as it gets.

Celebrity Quarter Horse Lovers

Many celebrities have fallen for the Quarter Horse's distinct charms. Most country and western music stars who ride do so on Quarter Horses. Model Christie Brinkley, former San Francisco 49er Joe Montana, and singer Jewel all own Quarter Horses. Billy Crystal, who wasn't a rider until he starred in the film *City Slickers*, was so enamored with his equine costar, Beechnut, that he purchased the horse after

The trail class event requires the American Quarter Horse to be light, responsive, and obedient for its rider.

filming was completed. This horse accompanied him to the Academy Awards, where Crystal rode him onstage before his monologue.

Famous American Quarter Horses

Doc's Keepin' Time: this black Quarter Horse has had several key film and television roles, with his most notable performance in the latest version of the film *Black Beauty*. Originally a race horse, but too slow to be in the money, Doc's Keepin' Time became one of the top equine entertainment stars. With many different tricks and stunts to his credit, he also appeared in the film *The Horse Whisperer* as Gulliver, was the rearing horse in the Busch beer advertisements, and had the recurring role of The Black in the children's television series, *The Black Stallion*.

Hightower: This unregistered Quarter Horse had the lead role of Pilgrim in the Robert Redford film *The Horse Whisperer*. Originally a western horse, Hightower appeared in English tack and was ridden hunt seat for the movie's first scenes before Pilgrim's accident. Hightower wore special makeup to depict Pilgrim's injuries, and was trained to appear menacing for some scenes. Incidentally, there were a total of seventeen Quarter Horses used in Redford's film.

Plain Justin Bar: Anyone who watched the film *Dances with Wolves* fell in love with Cisco, the beautiful buckskin gelding Kevin Costner rode. Justin, as the horse is known, won the very first Silver Spur Award in 1991, given to registered Quarter Horses that have promoted the breed or enriched people's lives.

Dash For Cash: Dash For Cash was one of the best racing Quarter Horses in history, if not *the* best. The 1976-77 World Champion, foaled in 1973, became the all-time leading sire of racing Quarter Horses, with earners of more than $39 million. During a career spanning three years and twenty-five starts, he won twenty-one races. Dash For Cash was the first horse to win the Champion of Champions title back to back, and the first horse in two decades to be named World Champion in consecutive years.

THE AMERICAN SADDLEBRED

HOW WOULD YOU CRAFT A HORSE? Make him beautiful and elegant—a true class act? Would he be athletic and expressive with every step he took? Or would you simply concoct a horse that loves your companionship? The creators of the American Saddlebred developed an animal that exhibits all these qualities, and more. With high-stepping, graceful action that comes naturally, complemented by a shining coat of burnished chestnut, bay, black, gray, palomino, or even pinto, the American Saddlebred is an elegant horse with a commanding presence in the show arena. Sometimes called the "peacock of the show ring," the Saddlebred serves up a healthy portion of fire and flash with its exaggerated, high-stepping action. Its flair comes from its past, when plantation owners in the South needed a horse to carry them comfortably yet stylishly across the fields and into town. Today you'll find the Saddlebred strutting its stuff in many equestrian events, from working cattle to performing delicate dressage maneuvers.

Breed History

It was the late 1700s in New England, and the British colonists needed to produce a horse suitable for their new environment. Crossing imported stock with sturdy Canadian horses, they created a horse that paced or ambled, a horse that would become the fountainhead for many American breeds. This easy-gaited horse, the Narragansett Pacer, was named for the bay in area Rhode Island from where it sprung.

It was not destined to exist as a pure strain for very long. Through short-sighted cross-breeding and exporting of animals, the Narragansett itself eventually

The Saddlebred's swanlike neck gives the horse a graceful air.

disappeared from American shores, though its blood continues to course through the veins of many American breeds even today.

By the time of the American Revolution, the colonists had crossed the tall, refined English Thoroughbred with the Narragansett, creating a lean, elegant mount possessing smooth, floating gaits. It was known throughout the colonies simply as the American Horse.

But could this horse be considered a type, or merely a crossbred? More colonists began singing the praises of this American Horse with the fancy movement and elegant poise. Soon, any doubt was dispelled when, in 1776, in a letter to the Continental Congress, a diplomat living in France requested this graceful, animated equine as a gift for Marie Antoinette. This call for the American Horse secured its place as a true type.

The early nineteenth century saw the American Horse taking on additional important roles. As the young nation developed, the horse helped new Americans head west. Kentucky plantation owners sought to refine the breed so that it was a smooth-moving, yet flashy, partner. It developed into the Kentucky Saddler. The Saddler became a regular sight along the lush, tree-lined roads of Kentucky, where plantation owners would trot their graceful mounts under a canopy of shade all afternoon to reach the next farm.

This horse was a delightful solution to their needs. It possessed flowing gaits so that farmers could ride in comfort from field to field, yet was solid and hardy enough for moderate farm work. Thoroughbred blood continued to infuse the breed, and the Kentucky Saddler became the American Saddlebred Horse—larger in stature, yet still maintaining its easy, smooth gaits. With each new infusion of blood, the horse displayed more versatility, and farmers enjoyed pitting one horse against another in weekend match races. Farm horse, riding partner, racehorse—the American Saddlebred Horse was a coveted creature, to be sought after.

Despite the breed's reputation as a flashy saddleseat mount, some American Saddlebreds make their way into the jumping arena.

*E*ven Saddlebred foals demonstrate their signature regal presence from the start.

The nation's volatile history became a proving ground for both Americans and their horses. During the Civil War, Saddlebreds could be found on both sides of the battlefield. Once the Civil War was over, the American Saddlebred still had much to offer its American breeders. America looked to show its prosperity, and horse shows and fairs quickly gained popularity. The first National Horse Show was held at the St. Louis Fair in 1856 and, in myriad classes, the American Saddlebred reigned supreme. It seemed easy for these lovely horses to impress the judges, and they walked, trotted, and cantered away with nearly all the prizes.

Thirty years later, special classes were developed so the breed's gifts would be more aptly put to the test. Saddle horses would be required to show at the trot in addition to the "saddle gaits" which at the time were the rack, running walk, fox trot—a gait where the horse trots in front while walking with its hind end—and slow pace—an ambling, single-foot gait.

Quality of gait and movement became a driving force for registering these horses—so much so that each horse had to perform its saddle gaits before registration was allowed. A stallion named Denmark, born in 1839, was designated the foundation sire; today more than 60 percent of Saddlebreds can trace their pedigrees back to him.

The registry, called The American Saddlebred Horse Association (ASHA), was founded in 1891 in Louisville, Kentucky—the first-ever breed association designated for an American horse. At that time, the horse was still more often found in a working capacity than as a show specimen, but that was soon to change.

Shortly before the twentieth century, both Americans and foreigners abroad were discovering the many talents of the American Saddlebred in the show ring. In 1893, at the St. Louis National Horse Show, a stallion as black as midnight entered the show arena. The crowd was amazed at his class, his animation, his regal bearing, and his beautiful conformation. Crowned as champion, Rex McDonald, the jet-black stallion, reigned for several years thereafter.

Show horses converged on the United States show scene, whether they were the posh events of New York and Los Angeles, the great state fairs of the South and Midwest, or the county fairs which were more often athletic contests than society functions. Agriculture was still the mainstay of America, and most Americans understood and appreciated the athleticism and splendor of these animals.

Although World War II had quelled some interest in horses and showing, in the late 1940s they returned with a vengeance. Suddenly, Saddlebreds were back in action, with some of the breed's top horses gracing the show ring, among them Wing Commander, six-time World's Grand Champion, and Oak Hill Chief, who was one of the first truly big stars. From rural areas to the big cities, Saddlebreds were becoming big entertainment—and big money for some trainers.

Breed Characteristics

The Saddlebred places high on the list of the world's most elegant horses, and whether you see one in the show ring or gliding down a trail, it's apparent that this horse has charisma. Its long, lean appearance is the result of careful breeding that strives for a

refined, stylish animal. But this is no hot-house flower. It is an athlete with tremendous potential.

The ideal American Saddlebred is well proportioned and presents an exquisite overall portrait. It is slender, though not thin, with good muscle tone, and a smooth, burnished coat. The average height is 15 to 16 hands, and the average weight is 1,000 to 1,200 pounds. All colors are acceptable; the most prominent are chestnut, bay, brown, and black, with some gray, roan, palomino, and pinto. Stallions should have a masculine presence and mares a pretty, feminine air.

With a refined head, expressive eyes, and an upright, swanlike neck, the Saddlebred's appearance exudes fire and excitement. Most are rather narrow through the chest, and have clean legs, and flexible, long pasterns that lead to well-formed, sound feet which often are trimmed long to accentuate the horse's movement. Sporting well-sprung ribs and a strong back, the croup of the Saddlebred is level with the tail.

Saddlebred shows offer classes in country pleasure and western pleasure in addition to the gaited events.

For the gaited classes in the show ring, the tail is set artificially high by a device called a tail set. This props the tail up when the animal is not in the show ring. Other artificial methods of setting tails include surgery.

The Saddlebred is shown in either three- or five-gaited classes under saddle, and in fine-harness classes. Three-gaited horses are judged at the walk, trot, and canter, where the horse's conformation, behavior and action are paramount. It executes all gaits in a collected, yet animated manner, with high elevation. The five-gaited Saddlebred is shown in the same three natural gaits, but also has two additional gaits enhanced by training—the slow gait and the rack. Both are four-beat gaits, like the walk, with the slow gait performed by moving almost in a prancing motion, lifting each leg high and hesitating in the air momentarily, before setting it down. The rack is a faster version of the slow gait: using a ground-covering stride, the horse snaps its knees and hocks up quickly as each foot leaves the ground at a different interval. Fine-harness horses are shown at an animated walk and a park trot, in which the horse snaps up the front legs and extends them outwards before setting them down.

Sports and Specialties

Saddlebreds are known for being the epitome of the flashy park horse, one that demonstrates outstanding refinement and elegance, manners, expression, and brilliant gaits. With their friendly, intelligent nature, they are popular as parade horses and police mounts. Some are successful hunters and jumpers; others have been known to barrel race. The Saddlebred's newest calling, however, is in dressage because of its animation and naturally elevated forehand.

Saddlebreds can be seen taking beginner riders around at neighborhood schooling shows, and in small unrated events that let novices acquire experience in a more competitive environment. But up the ladder of competition are a variety of major shows and state fairs where the cream of the crop compete for championship titles—and often big money. The Kentucky State Fair, held in August in Louisville, is considered the top championship show, and year in and year out, the American Royal in Kansas City, Missouri crowns many champions in their finals.

What makes a champion Saddlebred, then? Enthusiasts of the breed refer to a winning horse possessing "bloom"—which you might also describe as having

Five-gaited horses are shown with full manes and perform the rack and slow gait in addition to the walk, trot, and canter.

presence, or class. The horse also must be able to perform its gaits with elegance and energy. A five-gaited horse must exhibit this not only at the traditional gaits of walk, trot, and canter, but also perform the slow gait and rack with the utmost brilliance. Not every Saddlebred is cut out for the exacting five-gaited division, but that doesn't mean the horse won't be just fine in the three-gaited or fine-harness divisions.

It's quite a sight to see a five-gaited horse in the ring, with its full, lush mane flowing, just a touch of thin, braided ribbons added to the forelock and mane. These horses are competed with a high tail carriage, while the occasional false tailpiece,

COMPARABLE BREED

The Hackney is a fine harness horse that has its roots in Great Britain. At one time, Hackneys were popular for pulling carriages in everyday life. This refined, elegant little horse possesses brilliant action similar to the Saddlebred's, and also is considered a park horse. The Hackney Pony shares the studbook of the Hackney Horse, though it is smaller in stature. Both have high-stepping animation, an alert, refined appearance, and uphill conformation.

called "switches," may be added to enhance its fullness and length. Tails may be set or unset, but currently show competitors desire their horses' tails be set vertically. Because the rack is such an animated gait, and the back hoofprints overtake the front, five-gaited horses wear protective coverings called quarter boots on their front feet to protect against possible injury.

Three-gaited horses show off their elegant walk, trot, and canter. They are judged on the quality of their gaits and also how beautiful, refined and animated they are. Three-gaited horses have their manes completely roached, or shorn off, and the long tail hairs at the base of the dock are also trimmed short.

Fine-harness horses get to display their lovely walk and trot gaits. If they break into a canter they are penalized, but there's plenty of action in their lofty, airy movement. These horses also have boots on their front feet—mostly for fashion, not function—and sport full manes, tails, and ribbons.

There is also a pleasure division in Saddlebred shows. These classes emphasize the manners of the horse. Above all, the winning horse must appear to be a pleasure to work, whether it's in a five-gaited or a driving class.

It's all well and good to be judged among your peers, but even in open competition, you will see Saddlebreds in a variety of events—and not even know it. Against the European breeds in the dressage arena, many have been mistaken for

Imperator, a champion Saddlebred who spent his last years retired at Lexington's Kentucky Horse Park, had classic conformation, presence, and movement.

*T*oday many dressage riders are finding the talents of the Saddlebred suited to their sport.

warmbloods. Saddlebreds have been mistaken for Thoroughbred crosses when seen on the hunt field, the cross-country course, or in the show-jumping arena. Some have even been known to have "cow sense" and have made good partners in cutting and roping. More and more people are also discovering that the American Saddlebred makes a sure-footed trail partner and friend.

Famous Saddlebreds

History has played host to a great many Saddlebreds. In addition to the illustrious Morgans, Thoroughbreds, and now extinct Narragansett Pacers that for hundreds of years contributed their bloodlines to the development of this very American breed, this horse has served its country well. The most vivid example was its role in the Civil War, when top generals on both sides commanded from the backs of Saddlebreds, some of whom, most notably General Robert E. Lee's beloved gray, **Traveler,** became legendary. And Confederate General Stonewall Jackson had **Little Sorrel,** his chosen mount. On the Union side was Ulysses S. Grant and his horse Cincinnati.

Film and television have long provided a familiar venue for the breed's talents. The Saddlebred **Highland Dale** lived on a farm in Missouri and was only eighteen months old when he was discovered by Ralph McCutcheon, a trainer of animal motion picture stars. He went on to be cast as Fury in the western series of the same name that ran on NBC in the late 1950s and early 1960s. Highland Dale also starred in a version of *Black Beauty,* and was the black horse in the film *Giant,* starring Elizabeth Taylor and James Dean.

Mr. Ed, one of the most famous American Saddlebreds, started out as a parade and show horse named Bamboo Harvester. Born in California in 1949, he was purchased by the Mister Ed Company, which was owned by the president of California's Palomino Society, and went on to become the most famous television horse in America.

Celebrity Saddlebred Enthusiasts

Probably the most vocal supporter of the Saddlebred comes from the entertainment industry. William Shatner, who played James T. Kirk in the original *Star Trek,* has often been referred to as an ambassador for the breed. Shatner rode his American Saddlebred mare Great Belles of Fire in the film *Star Trek: Generations.* In 1994, as Grand Marshal of the Pasadena Rose Parade, Shatner rode I Prefer Montana, a half brother to this mare.

When not acting, directing, producing, and writing, Shatner is a successful horse breeder and competitor. He bred and owned world champion Sultan's Great Day. He also has proven to be an extremely accomplished rider, holding several championships in both indoor and outdoor American amateur competitions.

In addition to his tireless efforts on behalf of several charities, Shatner continues to host what has become an annual event—The Hollywood Charity Horse Show Reining Royals—which benefits several children's charities.

AMERICAN WHITE AND AMERICAN CREME

WHITE HAS OFTEN BEEN USED AS A SYMBOL of all that is good and pure—embodying the hero, in every sense. In the old westerns, the good guys always wore white, while the villains were clothed in black. It made it easier for us to know who to root for. Take the Lone Ranger, for example. In his white hat and with his gallant steed Silver, he personified goodness and justice.

Painters in the Middle Ages often portrayed their noble subjects mounted on white horses. Centuries ago, gallant white chargers were often the preferred mounts for battle.

Given that, throughout history, white animals have stood for good luck, purity, and fortune, is it any wonder people also wanted white horses in their lives? And so it is with American breeders who have worked diligently to produce horses pure as snow.

When most people think of a white horse, they assume that he's an albino. But the term albino is being used less often, because technically it's incorrect. Albinism is caused by the meeting of two recessive genes—the offspring inherits one recessive gene from each parent—and the gene that causes albinism has not been found to occur in equines.

Breed History

There are certain white horses that will be termed Albinos because they are registered with the International Albino Association in Naper, Nebraska. But these horses are actually American Whites, or American Cremes.

At the beginning of the twentieth century, a snow-white, pink-skinned, brown-eyed foal was born. Named Old King, he was owned by Caleb and Hudson

American whites and cremes can come in any breed, including draft horses.

Thompson, who used this horse as a breeding stallion. Old King was able to pass along his beautiful and unusual coat color to other generations, and the result would become the American Whites. The mares Old King was bred to were often of Morgan breeding, which is somewhat ironic, since Justin Morgan, the foundation stallion, was a dark bay.

In addition to their intriguing white coloring, the horses were also very talented and athletic. The Thompsons put together a White Horse Troupe, and began touring the country and Canada with their exhibition. Audiences fell in love with these dazzling white horses that performed as a finely-tuned team. Many were put in films, where they lit up the silver screen in various old-time westerns.

While the White Horse Troupe members, along with the rest of the Thompson stock, were of a more stocky, all-around western horse type, they weren't limited to just toiling on the ranch, or performing at rodeos and events. They also worked as dude ranch horses for kids, and even jumped, and performed in parades.

In 1937, Cal and his wife Ruth decided to found a registry for their beloved white horses. Their American

An American White was called an Albino until only a few years ago—a misnomer that still occasionally is used today.

Albino Horse Club offered registry for the sons and daughters of Old King, as well as other horses that met the coloration criteria. Their mission was to collect, preserve, and verify the pedigrees of these horses and to promote an interest in the various types of American Albino. Later, they added a division for horses with light cream or ivory coats.

White Horse Ranch became the official headquarters of the Albino Horse Club, which later changed its name to International American Albino Association (IAAA), yet remained a working breeding facility.

A White or Creme horse can be of any breed, and can come in any size or conformation. It can be double-registered, having an original pedigree with its breed association, and also be registered as a "color" horse.

American Cremes are more plentiful than their pure white cousins. American Whites remain a rarity and are quite expensive on the international front.

Breed Characteristics

Not all white horses are created equal. Even though a horse may look white, he still has to meet the genetic criteria of the association to be registered. IAAA horses must be born white or cream-colored. Thus, they are different from gray horses, which are usually born in a darker shade, such as chestnut, or even near-black, and whiten with age. The skin underneath must be pink, also different from that of gray horses, which have dark skin under their white coats. A White horse also has a white mane and tail, although their eyes can be brown, blue, or any color commonly found in horses. Contrary to popular belief, there has yet to be a true pink-eyed, pink-skinned, albino horse.

A Creme horse may be nearly white, but will never have that brilliant, clean white look. It is like comparing wedding dresses in ivory and white. In fact Creme horses can have variations, from rather light, to an almost palomino color. They often are born slightly deeper in color and lighten within the first year. A Creme can have white markings, such as stockings, a star, or a blaze, but these are so faint that they are visible only when the coat is wet. Their manes can be the same color as their coat, or can even be slightly darker. Their skin must be either pink or various shades of tan, but never gray. Their eyes are most often lighter than those of White horses, in shades like amber or light blue.

The American Creme sports a milky-colored coat with a slightly darker pink skin underneath.

One myth that is constantly being dispelled by enthusiasts of the breed is the notion that white animals are somehow weaker than their colored brethren. Since the horses aren't true albinos, nothing could be further from the truth. In fact these White and Creme horses, since they come from all walks of life, are versatile and talented in many areas. Although still very unusual to see at an open horse show, when a White or Creme is on display in reining, dressage, jumping, or driving, they simply sweep the audience off its collective feet. While the IAAA continues to strive toward a breed show program where Whites and Cremes come together to meet and compete with the best of their own association, the registry prefers it when the horses compete on the open circuit. They feel that when the world sees Whites and Cremes competing against their darker cousins, it helps generate excitement and enthusiasm. And since people occasionally have a few preconceived notions about the horses until they actually see them in action, the horses usually end up changing minds and attitudes.

Not all breed associations allow White and Creme horses into their registries, even if the horse is pure of blood. There are white American Saddlebreds, Walking Horses, Fox Trotters, Quarter Horses, Arabians, and pony breeds, for example, but some are not allowed dual registry, as a few unenlightened associations still believe the myth that white horses are genetically weaker. But they are truly missing out on something wonderful, since Whites and Cremes are often noted for their even tempers, talent, and longevity, with many living into their thirties.

This doesn't mean that White horses are completely without any special care, because they do require a bit of TLC to keep them not only brilliant white, but also healthy. For instance, they won't go blind out in the sunlight, but like any pale individual's, their pink skin can sunburn if left unprotected too long. Moderate exposure to sun keeps them healthy and happy.

It's hard to think that with the legends surrounding white horses, many people today still have a prejudice against them. But the noble white steed from fairy tale and folklore is a living, breathing creature that a fortunate, select few are able to enjoy in today's real world.

Famous Whites and Cremes

The most famous white horse people immediately think of is **Silver,** the Lone Ranger's horse. However, debate rages as to whether the horse was gray with dark skin; white with pink skin; or creme with dark skin. Tennessee Walking Horse historians claim that Silver was a Creme Walker.

Napoleon was said to be a lover of white horses—and some accounts say that he owned fifty of them. Whether they were gray horses or white with pink skin remains a mystery.

White Thoroughbreds are rare, but they do occur occasionally. The first registered white Thoroughbred in America, a filly named **White Beauty,** was born at Patchen Wilkes Farm in 1963 and gained national attention for her blazing white coat.

More recently, **Patchen Beauty,** White Beauty's great-granddaughter, a white Thoroughbred mare, caused a stir when she competed on the Kentucky circuit in the mid–1990s. She had two victories and earned nearly $55,000 during her career—and she has a fan club. Her owners decided she would not be raced in claiming races, because people wanted to buy her strictly because of her beautiful coat. When she was seven years old, she was used as a broodmare and delivered a white foal, a colt named **The White Fox,** just like herself.

THE APPALOOSA

INDIAN PONY—THE VERY TERM CONJURES UP images of the Old West. We picture horses, adorned with an assortment of war paint patterns, charging into canyons at a full gallop, and chasing buffalo with their bareback riders astride. Today, those legendary horses still exist—born of special Native American breeding. The Appaloosa, a treasure from yesteryear, bears its own unique markings—not needing extra adornment from its master. The horse's colorful coat, along with its expressive face and willing nature, have made it a cherished friend to many Appy lovers—even though man has not always been kind to this true native jewel.

Breed History

Spotted horses did not start with the Appaloosa. We have to go much further back in the annals of history, to prehistoric times, to places where the world was still icy and inhospitable. Cave dwellers, living in what is now known as Europe, adorned their lodging walls with the images of spotted horses. Spotted horse evidence is also found from 1500 B.C., in the steppe region of central Asia, and even in Persia, where the spotted horse Rakush was revered as a war mount by Ferdowsi, in his epic poem c. 1000 A.D.

Centuries later, in Denmark and Austria, horses with small, circular patches of color on a base coat were specifically bred. Andalusians and Lippizzan horses of the sixteenth century bore spotted patterns, too. It was these horses, most likely, that accompanied New World explorers on their travels. Like many of the European horses that made it to American shores, some escaped, others were lost, and some were stolen by natives who were captivated by their beautiful coat patterns.

The costume class, part of the Appaloosa's native heritage, is still celebrated today in competition.

Although most tribes in the Pacific Northwest had working horses by the turn of the eighteenth century, one tribe in particular emerged as expert horsemen. They were the Nez Percé, and they called the area around Oregon and Washington home. Skilled riders, they were even more adept at bringing out the best in horses by practicing selective breeding. No mediocre stock was allowed—only the finest of their herd were used to carry on and improve the next generation. A horse that was not swift, colorful, and beautiful would be gelded, or traded to other tribes. Those that remained strengthened the Nez Percé herd, producing even more hardy, athletic equines. From their straight profiles, to their slightly arched, upright necks, to their powerful hindquarters, the Appaloosa bespoke both beauty and power. Their legs became stronger and their hooves harder. Their tails and manes became sparse, so that they wouldn't catch on brush and brambles. The spots not only served as coveted and distinctive markings, they also worked as an intricate camouflage, to better hide from prey or foe. Their numbers soared into the thousands, and they were treasured by their keepers.

In the late 1800s, white settlers began their trek west, staking their claim to the untamed lands. The spotted mount of the Indians became known as "A Palouse" horse, named for the Palouse River that ran through the area. The U.S. government decided to take this land for its citizens by displacing the native peoples and putting them onto reservations. Wars between the U.S. government and various native tribes broke out. In 1877, it was the Nez Percé's turn to fight for freedom.

The stamina and strength of the hardy Appaloosa thwarted the U.S. Cavalry for months as Chief Joseph and his Nez Percé tribe fled more than thirteen hundred miles in an effort to avoid capture. Young and old, women and children, boys and men

Appaloosa coats don't necessarily have to have loud spots. This roan Appaloosa has a slight dusting of white over its topline.

*L*ike a Dalmatian, a leopard Appaloosa has large dark spots covering its white body.

were forced to cross rivers, scale mountainous terrain, and traverse the expansive Northwestern plains on their way to their final goal: Canada. It was a harsh, unforgiving journey, and numerous tribe members and horses succumbed along the way. Finally, Chief Joseph's tribe was overtaken, just short of the Canadian border—and their possible freedom. The weather was frigid, the losses had been many, the suffering great. Overwhelmed, the great chief surrendered, saying "I will fight no more forever."

The Cavalry then issued an edict: kill every one of the spotted horses, the Palouse horses, or Appaloosas, as they were now called. It would ensure that the Nez Perce would never be able to escape again. What better way to subdue the tribe than to destroy its most prized possession? The beautiful, colorful, unique horses were methodically trapped and shot. Within a short time, their numbers dwindled, although some managed to escape into the hills. Regrettably, the U.S. Cavalry gelded most stallions, the premium stock. A handful were kept secretly by settlers and ranchers as saddle mounts. These Appaloosas were crossed with draft or Spanish mares to produce stock to work their farms. The pure race of Appaloosas seemed all but gone.

Student Francis Haines attempted to tell the world in 1937 that the Appaloosa was not merely an Indian prize but an American treasure. He wrote his doctoral thesis about the Nez Percé history and documented the vengeful act the U.S. Military had carried out.

Only a few hundred horses remained—including those carefully hidden by Oregon rancher Claude Thompson. He read Haines's report, and he and others decided to take matters into their own hands. Along with a handful of dedicated breeders, they joined together to form a group that would protect and promote the Appaloosa. The next year, in 1938, the Appaloosa Horse Club (ApHC) was founded in Moscow, Idaho—near where the breed originated. Members of the group went on a quest to find remaining living horses to become the foundation stock. They first attempted to refine the draft/farm Appaloosa crosses, choosing to use Arabian blood. Later, Quarter Horses were blended with the Appaloosas to broaden the gene pool and regain more of the original conformation. Slowly, the breed came back from the brink.

The next few decades saw an increase in numbers. As popularity grew in the 1970s and 1980s, the Appaloosa was counted among America's favorite stock breeds.

But what makes an Appaloosa an Appaloosa? Over the years, its registry allowed certain breeds into its studbooks to infuse it with outside blood, strengthening and changing the breed. And while many resulting Appys bear the characteristics of their forefathers, there are a good deal that do not. They may be solid-colored horses. Or they may be spotted, but their conformation is nothing like the old-style Appaloosa. Because of ample outcrossing with American Quarter Horses, Arabians, and Thoroughbreds, some breed purists—the foundation stock lovers—are critical of the fact that this practice still exists. Why? The characteristics that make the Appaloosa so special—the spots, the striped hooves, the white sclera around the eye, and the mottled skin—are diminished, and often it becomes difficult to tell this remarkable horse from so many others.

Breed Characteristics

Like fingerprints, no two Appaloosas are alike—in color or conformation. Depending on the horse's genetic background, the horse can have a somewhat muscular build and more upright carriage, denoting its foundation blood. Or it can be even bulkier, reflecting its Quarter Horse ancestry. The leaner, sporthorse type often has Thoroughbred blood coursing through its veins. They can be anywhere from 14.2 to 16 hands in height, with a small, well-formed profile, and pointed ears. The horse has expressive, almost human eyes, due in part to the white sclera that rings the eye. The Appaloosa is known for having tough-as-nails feet and often does not require shoes. It has a nice slope to its shoulder, a deep chest, and good bone underneath it. Many Appaloosas' hooves show contrasting light and dark vertical stripes. Another characteristic of the breed is mottled, freckly skin around the muzzle and genitals.

The Appaloosa has several color patterns, from the sublime to the outlandish. Some horses have a snowflake pattern, in which a solid coat looks sprinkled with a healthy dusting of white. A leopard bears its spots like a fireman's Dalmatian. An Appaloosa wearing a blanket has a solid white area resting on his hips or even up to his shoulder, and often there are darker spots found within the blanket. Some are even roan, but it's a distinctive pattern, complete with dark strips along the facial bones, known as "varnish."

And as individual as these horses are, so are their talents. No longer seen just as ranch horses or Indian ponies, the Appaloosa can be found in a variety of events and riding styles. New breed associations have even developed to support the horse

The Appaloosa sport horse is becoming more sought after in the disciplines of dressage and show jumping.

in Olympic disciplines, calling on the Appaloosa Sport Horse Association to help usher the breed into open events such as combined training, dressage and show jumping. These horses are showing that their beauty is not just skin deep. Dressage is a sport that is as exacting as it is physically demanding, but the Appaloosa is one American breed that is seen in levels all the way up to Grand Prix.

Appaloosas can also turn on the speed when called upon. Appaloosa racing is found along the American West Coast, where horses as lean and nearly as swift as racing Thoroughbreds pound the racetracks.

More Appys are being found in events that require significant stamina, including endurance, competitive trail riding, and the three-day event. With their legendary soundness and good wind, they can go the distance for their riders easily.

Despite their wild color, Appaloosas are prized for their calm, temperate dispositions, and you'll often find them to be good horses for novices. The breed can also

This classic blanket-patterned Appaloosa features a few large oblong spots over the large splash of white on his rump.

COMPARABLE BREED

The Knabstrupper, a loudly spotted, colored warmblood from Denmark, is a rare equine, but Danish breeders are working to diligently produce more for riding and sport. Like the Appaloosa, these horses have an even temper and an intelligent mind, are quick to learn, and exhibit a willing nature. Their spotted coats have many different colors and variations, from leopard to blanket-patterned.

be seen in a variety of jobs that call for an easygoing temperament, including dude ranch mount, lesson horse, and child's first horse.

Each year around November, the Appaloosa Horse Club sponsors the Appaloosa World Show, held at the Will Rogers Equestrian Center in Fort Worth, Texas. Appaloosas show off their talents in just about every class imaginable. There are traditional rail classes, such as western pleasure, equitation, western riding, and hunter under saddle, as well as in-hand classes like yearling longe-line, halter, and showmanship. Cow classes, such as roping, steer daubing, cutting and working cow horse, highlight the breed's past as a valued ranch horse. Gymkhana events, such as the keyhole race, the rope race, and the Nez Percé stakes race, celebrate the breed's native traditions.

The ApHC also offers heritage classes at the World Show, featuring Appaloosas and their riders dressed in costumes that relate to the breed's history.

Famous Appaloosas

Probably the most recognizable Appaloosa today is **Bright Zip,** riding and clinician partner of John Lyons, known as "America's Most Trusted Horseman." Bright Zip was the first horse to be inducted into the Appaloosa Horse Club Hall of Fame while still alive. Bright Zip lost his sight in 1995, due to a reaction to an injection, yet continued to attend symposiums and events with Lyons across the country.

A famous racehorse on the Appaloosa circuit was **Apache Double.** Burning up the track in the 1970s, this running Appaloosa set speed records that still remain unbroken.

For the sporthorse world, **Wap Spotted** is a recognizable name. In the 1990s this stallion helped create a new and very competitive athlete in a time when warmbloods and solid-colored horses were *de rigueur.* The foundation stallion of the Appaloosa Sport Horse Association, Wap Spotted founded a lineage that continues to influence Appaloosa sporthorse breeding, and his offspring are found performing in both jumping and dressage. While he was only shown for two seasons on the prestigious hunter/jumper A-circuit, his legacy is in his progeny, which have won championships in the English disciplines that are normally ruled by solid-colored warmbloods and Thoroughbreds.

Today's Appaloosa is found in every riding discipline, and with all kinds of owners, from beginners to international competitors. While many types have been bred to suit specific sports, you'll still find a few Appaloosas harking back to the days when their swift hooves carried them across the Pacific Northwest, a true partner to those who loved them best.

Many Appaloosas are at home in western events, such as the trail class.

THE AZTECA

AZTECA: WITH A NAME LIKE THAT the horse must have come from south of the border, a horse of Mexico, right? Many would wonder why the Azteca, which did in fact originate in Central America, might also be thought of as an American breed. The answer lies in the fact that this breed is relatively new on the scene—less than three decades in existence. Additionally, while its origin is in Mexico, half of its foundation lies in North America, with the Quarter Horse.

Considered the National Horse of Mexico since 1972, the Azteca is the result of Andalusian—which, ironically, is not a native Mexican breed either—and Quarter Horse breeding, with the ideal Azteca bearing five-eighths Spanish horse blood, the remainder being Quarter Horse. In Mexico, three generations of Azteca-to-Azteca breedings are common, while in the United states, an Azteca can be a first-generation cross-bred and still be registered.

The Azteca Horse Registry of America was formed in 1989, and its sister organization, the Azteca Horse Owners Association, started in 1996.

Breed History

There are early references that the Conquistadors' horses were Hacas, a hardy breed of horse similar to today's Andalusian, from Spain. These Hacas were said to have been turned loose by the Conquistadors to roam free in Mexico, rather than taken back on the long journey to Spanish shores. The free Hacas migrated up through the Southwestern area of America, where they were captured and trained by the native peoples for hunting buffalo and for battle. When Spaniards returned to the West Coast to establish their missions and create settlements, they brought with

Gray is dominant in the Azteca breed, although today there are more animals bred in a variety of colors.

them additional horses. These horses bore the *Pura Raza Espanol* bloodlines—the pure Spanish race—and were known as being of three main types: the Haca, the Andalusian, and the Lusitano of Portugal. All three had amazing cow sense, having been bred over generations for bullfighting in Spain and Portugal. Some of these Spanish horses ended up in the Quarter Horse and American Paint Horse gene pools.

From those Spanish bloodlines, the American Quarter Horse had inherited a natural cow savvy. When Andalusians became more popular in the late 1970s and 1980s in America and Mexico, breeders became interested in adding back some of that Spanish blood to the Quarter Horse breed.

It's easy to see that the American Quarter Horse is an athlete—especially when it comes to working cattle. But after breeding Quarter Horses to the very graceful and agile Andalusian, breeders were thrilled with the outcome, and began to breed this combination in earnest, calling it the Azteca. Some say that Mexican breeders added Criollo horses into the mix as well. The result is a horse that

The profile of the Azteca often shows the noble bloodlines of its Spanish ancestry.

COMPARABLE BREED

Since the Azteca gets so much of its presence from the Spanish horses, it's easy to see its similarity to the Lusitano, the Pura Raza Espanol horse of Portugal. With similar cow sense and gorgeous, animated gaits, and appearance, the Lusitano—like its cousin the Andalusian—is sought after by pleasure riders and competitors alike.

is able to execute intricate classical dressage movements, as well as deal with an errant cow on the ranch. They are intelligent, and the Quarter Horse blood gives them an extra infusion of level-headedness. Enthusiasts of the breed note that the Azteca is very people-oriented, and seem to prefer the company of their caretakers to that of the other horses in the herd. They are affectionate and willing to please, which makes training go all the more quickly.

A first-generation American Azteca registered in America is the result of crossing a registered Andalusian to a registered Quarter Horse. Subsequent generations may be bred back and forth as long as neither parent exceeds six-eighths of the whole.

Breed Description

The Azteca blends beautiful attributes of both its breeds into a magical alchemy. It is a medium-sized horse, standing about 15 to 16 hands tall at maturity. Like their Spanish-blooded Andalusian cousins, they are often born dark but then lighten and turn gray when they reach adulthood. For many years, Andalusians were most commonly gray, but more recently Andalusian breeders have sought to produce bay and black horses. Because of this, Aztecas are increasingly seen in a variety of coat colors. The legs are strong and dense, with hard, durable hooves that grow very slowly. They generally have an upright carriage due to a beautiful curved neck, and a close-coupled body, with full manes and tails. Their profile is generally straight.

Aztecas mature at a slower rate than their Quarter Horse relatives, and should not be ridden until they reach their third birthday. In fact, like many warmbloods, some don't completely mature until they are four years old—or even older. Because colts can be very obedient and calm, some owners wait until the horse is two years old before deciding to geld.

❶bedient and willing, the Azteca is cherished as a saddle horse

Although few have actually heard of the Azteca in North America, Mexico's affection for their national horse will certainly help speed up its recognition in the States. No matter what side of the border its owners are on, both agree that Aztecas are beautiful, kind, and athletic equines with a promising future in the world.

Famous Aztecas

Ramon Becerra, a trick horse trainer in Central California, uses several Azteca horses in his program.

THE BASHKIR CURLY

IMAGINE IF YOU WERE ALLERGIC TO HORSES: your favorite animal. It wasn't the hay or the straw in their stalls that made you miserable; it was their very coats. Your passion for horses, your love for riding—would you have to forever banish them from your life? American Bashkir Curly enthusiasts say: not necessarily.

American Bashkir Curlies are named after the Bashkir, an ancient breed of horse that hails from Russia; however, the association may be in name only. Curly-coated horses from the former Soviet Union are known as Lokai, not Baskhirs, although the occasional Russian Bashkir can be found with a curly coat. But it's pretty widely accepted among curly-coated horse enthusiasts that if a Russian Bashkir is curly, it's because it has Lokai blood in its ancestry. But what's in a name, really? What matters most is the unique horse, not its moniker.

Breed History

The American Curly was discovered living free in the deserts of Nevada, just before the turn of the twentieth century. A little boy named Peter Damele and his father were trail riding through the arid central Nevada foothills around the area known as Austin. They stopped in their tracks along the way, astounded to come across three feral horses with ripply, wavy rings of hair covering their bodies. They captured them and took them home to the Damele farm.

Many theories have sprung up to explain how these mysterious horses just happened to be found in this area of the West, but the fact is that no one quite knows their true origin. One is that the horses came from Russia across an ice bridge from the Bering Strait, but this notion is hardly likely. A more plausible

The mane of the American Bashkir Curly can have heavy ringlets or slight waves.

The close-coupled build of the Bashkir Curly, similar to the old-style Morgan horse, makes it maneuverable and agile.

theory is that Russian pioneers of the Pacific Northwest might have brought Curly horses with them to their new home. Some have speculated that a few of these horses escaped and joined other feral horses, then meandered down into California, ending their journey in Nevada. This trek would have been long and arduous, and nothing but the hardiest of horses would have had even a slim chance of coming out alive.

There is some evidence that curly-coated horses have been in North America for at least two hundred years. Pictographs drawn by Native Americans illustrating "winter counts" in 1801–1802 depict horses that look similar to Curlies being stolen from Crow tribes by the Sioux. Since curly coats have occasionally cropped up in feral South American horses as well, it's difficult to determine exactly how these three horses ended up right in front of the Dameles. Their precise origin may forever remain a mystery.

The American Bashkir Curly is able to pass along its characteristic coat about 50 percent of the time when crossed with a non-curly-coated horse. American Curly horses are sturdy creatures, able to withstand harsh climates and tough winters.

In 1971, the American Bashkir Curly Registry was created in order to recognize, preserve, and protect the breed. The horses have fans all over North America, thanks to their incredibly gentle, eager-to-please natures. They are excellent pleasure mounts, because they have sensible trail manners and good temperaments, but more are being found in the competition arena, particularly dressage.

Breed Description

Standing from 14.3 to about 15 hands high, the horse has a close-coupled, upright frame, reminiscent of old-school Morgans. They have well-proportioned heads with small ears, wide-set eyes, and usually straight profiles. Built uphill, with a rounded shoulder that springs from a slightly arched neck, Curly Horses have dense, round leg bone, hard, flinty hooves, and flat knees. The hindquarters are round, with powerful haunches, and the chest is wide. Because of the small gene pool, however, Curlies are being cross-bred with a variety of other breeds, resulting in Curlies of all sizes from draft horse to pony, and of every coat pattern and color, including Appaloosa and pinto.

But what is most unusual and intriguing about the Bashkir Curly is its silky, ringlet-covered coat. Their coats are known to be hypoallergenic, meaning that anyone allergic to the coat or scurf and dander of regular horses is less likely to be affected around the Bashkir Curly. Some horses are simply covered with wild tight waves, like a Rex breed of cat. Others are fairly slick-coated and their curls are much more subtle. Many Curlies' winter coats are thick and wavy in the cold months, but are lighter and easy to care for in the summertime. In winter a Curly will often shed its mane, and even tail hairs, only to grow them back come spring.

Proponents of the Curly enthuse about how easy the horse is to train. Many enjoy the complex nature of dressage, and adapt to the intricacies of the sport willingly. They also have wonderful endurance, and are well suited to competitive trail and

COMPARABLE BREED

The Russian Lokai, as mentioned, also has a natural curl to its coat. With a smaller and lighter build, the Lokai is a very uncommon breed.

endurance racing. Western speed events such as barrel racing, pole bending, and keyhole racing are also fun for riders to participate in. When matched together, Curlies make a great drill team or parade group, which helps garner more fans whenever they appear in public.

The horse is his own best advertisement. A person has but to see a Curly in action, and he or she will be curious and want to learn more about this fascinating, unusual equine. It's easy to see that there will be an increase in demand in the future, as more equestrians want to "ride the wave" of the Curly.

Famous Bashkir Curlies

Sunny Martin, founder of the American Bashkir Curly Registry and long-time breeder in Nevada, was asked to bring several Bashkir Curlies to the Tournament of Roses Parade in Pasadena in 1984. The group was asked back several more times for repeat appearances.

In 2002, the **Classic Curly Riders,** a team of eleven, represented the breed in the 113th Rose Parade, marking the seventeenth time that the breed had been featured in that event.

Sparlock, a tobiano-patterned Curly, has done very well in the sport of dressage. He competes at the upper levels, in competitions governed by international rules. This lovely mover has garnered championships at Fourth Level, and has also competed successfully in Intermediare I and II, with sights set at the top level, the Grand Prix.

Spartacus, a blue-gray pinto stallion, was Indiana State Reserve Champion Dressage Horse for three years, regional American Horse Shows Association (now known as USA Equestrian, or USAEq) Horse of the Year, and also won first place in Pinto as well as Bashkir Curly Breed Performance awards with the United States Dressage Federation (USDF).

THE CHINCOTEAGUE PONY

LOOK ON THE SHELF OF ANY HORSE LOVER—young or old—and you'll probably find a copy of Marguerite Henry's *Misty of Chincoteague*, which tells the true story of a brother and sister living off the coast of Virginia in the 1940s, and how they were caught under the spell of the wild ponies that roamed an island across the channel. No matter what part of the country they lived in, no matter what decade they read the book, it's safe to say most readers finished it with dreams of making a journey to the little island on the last Thursday in July to buy their very own Chincoteague Pony.

While some of the book is fanciful and other parts fact, we do know that the island ponies are very real—and very special.

Breed History

Assateague and Chincoteague Islands, located just on the ocean side of Chesapeake Bay, are known to have been home to feral horses since the 1700s. Small and hardy, the horses thrived in spite of extreme weather and limited vegetation, feeding on saltmarsh cordgrass and seaweed indigenous to the wind-whipped islands.

Legend has it that during the sixteenth century, a Spanish galleon carrying horses to the New World wrecked while coming ashore, and the horses spilled overboard, many swimming to the safety of Assateague Island. While this is the most romantic notion of how the ponies came to be, other theories based a little more in reality are probably more accurate. The horses were probably released into the wilds of Assateague in the seventeenth century by Virginia settlers, who wanted to avoid paying taxes on their livestock. Or they may have just been property of colonists

The Chincoteague Pony, although feral, has become accustomed to the encroachments of modern civilization.

who didn't have proper farms with fences, yet wanted to make sure their horses didn't escape into the Virginia hills. The horses were soon joined by other livestock, including cattle, sheep, and hogs.

In the 1700s, farmers decided to round up the horses so that they could work their land. They wanted to lay claim to the ponies quickly, so they put aside a day to "pen" the ponies, herding them up, then branding, and breaking them for work. This became a regular occasion, and by the late eighteenth century, penning not only of ponies, but of sheep, was held annually.

In the 1800s, the round up became more popular among Island residents. The whole island of Chincoteague looked forward to the day, turning penning into a festivity. The event became something of a tourist attraction, which was a boon for local businesses. In 1909, it was decided to set an annual date aside, and the last Wednesday and Thursday of July became official Pony Penning Days. Sheep penning, however, didn't fare as well in the hearts of locals and ceased to exist in 1914.

With other tourism helping the island's commerce year round, it became important to safeguard the well-being of visitors. After two tragic fires struck the islands in the 1920s, the Chincoteague Volunteer Fire Department was founded. They had the manpower, but still needed to find a way to keep this young department financially afloat. The answer was to take the money raised at pony penning and its accompanying Carnival and use it to purchase equipment and supplies for the fire department. The department in turn would be responsible for caring for the herd and overseeing the penning.

In the early 1920s, a wealthy farmer named Samuel Fields bought up a huge portion of Assateague—particularly at the southern end, known to be full of oysters. This forced many villagers to move to Chincoteague. It also changed the structure of pony penning, and in 1923, the event was moved to its permanent home on Chincoteague. The herds were at first transferred by boat, but in 1925 they were first swum across the narrow, shallow channel, and pony penning's "modern" era began. Tourists soon heard of the swimming ponies and began arriving from all over the nation for the annual penning. By the next decade, nearly twenty-five thousand tourists and residents were witness to this event.

The fire department took its new role as the ponies' caretaker seriously, and began monitoring their health and well-being. One area they were concerned about was the limited gene pool, since no new horses had been introduced to the herd for

Horse lovers young and old often dream of finding a horse or foal that looks like the famous Misty of Chincoteague.

generations. In 1939, the fire department set twenty Mustangs free on the island to breed with the ponies. Some years later, Arabian stock was also introduced to help bring back the herds' refined features, which had been diluted by the Mustang blood.

In 1943, Assateague Island was purchased by the federal government and divided into Assateague National Seashore Park and Chincoteague National Wildlife Refuge.

Pony Penning Days held in the last part of July have the ponies swim the shallow channel from their Assateague Island home to Chincoteague.

COMPARABLE BREED

The New Forest Pony from the southwest of England is probably the most genetically diverse of all native British ponies, due to "commoners" who lived in the forests being allowed to let their horses roam free. Like the Chincoteague, many different influences can be found in the New Forest gene pool. Also, like the American ponies, the New Forest Pony is annually rounded up and auctioned off.

The Chincoteague Volunteer Fire Department continued its job of caring for the ponies, and continued its annual pony-penning procedure. With all the money that came in from Pony Penning Days, the fire department completely upgraded its equipment and facilities. In 1947, the department sought out ponies that were locally owned, purchased them, and began their own fire department herd, which they moved to Assateague. After this time, the government no longer let locals graze their herds on Assateague, saving that privilege for only these publicly owned feral herds.

That same year, 1947, *Misty of Chincoteague* hit the bookstores. This tale traces the fanciful origins of the ponies, the Beebe children, the wild pony mare Phantom, and her spunky, quizzical foal Misty, and has become an award-winning classic, still enjoyed today by horse-crazy kids.

Chincoteague Island has become a tourist attraction for horse lovers around the world, who visit annually during summer to watch the pony penning and perhaps obtain a Chincoteague Pony of their own. To this day, the penning and festival are this area's biggest attractions. The Chincoteague Volunteer Firemen's Carnival starts well in advance, but the big days are in the last week. Thursday morning is the day of the swim. The start time has to be flexible because the event organizers want to ensure pony safety, and factors including tide, currents, and readiness of ponies, are considered.

Local ranchers and riders gain the title of "saltwater cowboys" during the event, as they gather up the ponies and herd them to shore to swim the narrowest part of Assateague Channel at low tide, beginning at Chincoteague Memorial Park, located on the east side of the island.

Upon their arrival on Chincoteague, the ponies are given a rest and a full examination by veterinarians to make sure that they weathered the swim in good form. Soon after, they make their way through town by trotting down roads that lead to a corral at the Carnival grounds, where they stay until the next day's auction.

The auction is the part that everyone is waiting for but folks can also grab a bite to eat in the dining room on Carnival grounds, served by the Ladies' Auxiliary, just as they have for decades. The fairground rides and games keep visitors in high spirits, and live music, and a raffle round out the Carnival's events. On Friday, the horses that weren't sold swim back to Assateague for another year of living free.

Interest in the ponies has increased in the last couple of decades, and because not everyone can make it to Virginia to buy a pony, Chincoteague lovers are starting up their own breeding operations, creating their domestic herds of Chincoteague Ponies from once feral ponies captured and sold at Penning Day. This has opened up a new world of opportunity for the Chincoteague, and as a result, they are showing up all over the country. Once thought of as a kid's pleasure pony, today's Chincoteague is being seen in the open show ring as a child's hunter or dressage mount, since they are willing and athletic. And some even appear in western and English pleasure classes. Their hardy nature makes them good western games ponies, too.

The most famous group of ponies is the ten-member Chincoteague Pony Drill Team, which performs at a variety of events, expos, and horse fairs. Audiences are always captivated by their precision movements and fun patterns as the ponies work in unison.

Breed Characteristics

For the most part, feral Chincoteague Ponies are bred through the process of natural selection. You'll see that there's quite a bit of variation in their breed characteristics, with all kinds of conformation, color, and bloodlines evident. There are signs of Welsh, Arabian, and Mustang influence, since these horses were put in to breed with the original feral herds.

Chincoteagues generally have a petite profile with wide-set eyes and a broad forehead. Some have Arabian-like dished faces, but occasionally the Mustang blood will come through for a more straight profile. They usually have a short,

Chincoteague Ponies are often a good choice for a child's first pony.

close-coupled body, with a good sloping shoulder, and round hindquarters. Their legs have good solid bone and tough hooves. Since breeding varies, they can be any size from 12 hands up to 14.2 hands, or taller. While pinto markings, made famous by Misty's "map of America" are common, you'll find ponies in nearly every coat color.

Their temperaments are very willing, and they are intelligent and eager to please.

There are two registries that serve the Chincoteague Pony, to preserve and protect the breed. The main requirement for registration is that all ponies be able to trace their lineage back to the island. Devotees needn't merely wish for an opportunity to travel to the Eastern Seaboard in order to find the pony of their dreams anymore. With its increasing numbers, the Pony may often find them.

Famous Chincoteague Ponies

Of course, the most famous pony of all is **Misty,** who did national tours in a traveling exhibit and met children from around the world until her death at twenty-six years of age in 1962. She can still be seen by all at the Misty Museum on Chincoteague Island—yes, stuffed, mounted, and on display.

Misty had several foals, including **Wisp o' Mist, Cyclone,** and **Phantom Wings.** But her most famous offspring was **Stormy,** who was featured in Marguerite Henry's *Stormy, Misty's Foal.* Stormy was born in horrific hurricane conditions that killed hundreds of wild Assateague ponies. Like her dam, she also became famous—and even gave birth to a foal that looked uncannily like Misty—so much so, that she was named **Misty II.**

THE COLORADO RANGER HORSE

IF YOU THINK APPALOOSAS ARE THE ONLY American horses with spots, think again. For while the Colorado Ranger Horse can have all the characteristics of its Appaloosa cousin, he's really "a horse of a different color." This breed's origin goes beyond American shores, tracing its beginnings to the blood of Middle Eastern horses.

Breed History

It all started with Ulysses S. Grant, the Union Civil War general who later went on to lead the country as president. Grant was an excellent horseman and always appreciated a good mount. Following his presidency, in 1877–1878 he sailed to Europe and the Middle East. He spent some time in Turkey, where he met the Sultan Hamid. Hamid and Grant developed an amicable relationship, and when Grant was ready to return home, Hamid sent with him a farewell gift of two young horses, an Arabian named Leopard and a Barb named Linden Tree. The gray stallions returned to America and became part of Grant's stable, where he used their Oriental bloodlines to help diversify his stock.

In 1879, the two stallions were loaned to Rudolf Huntington, a renowned breeder of trotting horses on the East Coast. For more than a decade, Leopard and Linden Tree were used in hopes of establishing a new line of trotters—which Huntington considered calling the Americo-Arab. For fourteen years, Huntington carefully pursued his dream of creating a new light-harness horse. Just before the turn of the century, Huntington lost the funding for his extensive breeding program. The two now rather aged stallions were put into breeding programs at the Colby ranch in Nebraska and also the A.C. Whipple family

The breed is known for having excellent cow sense, and therefore does well in working western events.

ranch in Colorado. In one mere breeding season, the two stallions made an impact on those breeding programs like no other horses. Covering mares that were basically range stock of mixed breeding, the horses surprised their breeders by siring foals with spots—full-blown Appaloosa markings. The foals grew up to have amazing cow sense as well. A new working cow horse was born, dubbed the Colorado Ranger.

But most of the first Rangerbred breeders didn't place that much emphasis on whether or not the horse had color, even though early foals quite often bore wild patterns and spots. Because the gene pool they were working with was small, linebreeding was common and Rangerbred horses seemed to come out with spots of all colors and patterns, including leopard, blanket, and snowflake.

Colorado State University became interested in the new Rangerbred and, with breeder Mike Ruby, helped fund a program to produce working horses. Ruby used two stallions, Patches #1 and Max #2, offspring from the Leopard and Linden Tree breedings.

Ruby's resulting crop of foals was amazingly consistent. The horses had the stamina and refinement of their Arabian and Barb ancestors. They also had a superior "cowy" nature and the level-headedness of their dams, the range mares. Throughout the early 1900s, Mike Ruby kept detailed records of the breeding and the foals that resulted. The horses were indeed good working cow horses and ranch stock, but they also drew much attention from regular horsemen. In 1938, the horse officially received its name as the Colorado Ranger Horse, and Mike Ruby founded the association that year.

Breed Characteristics

The Rangerbred is a medium-sized horse, standing anywhere from 14.2 to 16 hands high. It generally has stock-horse conformation, with a level topline, powerful haunches, clean legs, solid hooves, and smallish profile. And while one Appaloosa in eight also could be registered as a Rangerbred, it is not a color registry. Many registered Colorado Ranger Horses also bear solid coats. To meet the requirements for registration, a horse must

*T*he first Colorado Ranger Horse breeders didn't place much emphasis on color, although the horses often had loud spotted patterns, like Appaloosas.

Also known as a Rangerbred, the Colorado Ranger has typical stock horse conformation, with a level topline, beefy hindquarters, petite profile, and clean, straight legs.

show a direct descent from at least one of the two foundation stallions, Max #2 and Patches #1.

With a breed registry that is nearly three-quarters of a century old, one might think that there would be many more thousands of Rangerbred horses scattered across America, yet their numbers hover around six thousand. Today's Colorado Rangerbreds are registered with their breed association by meeting strict guidelines of particular bloodlines as well as conformation requirements. Outcrossings with Thoroughbreds, American Quarter Horses, Appaloosas, Arabians, and AraAppaloosas are allowed into the registry to keep the gene pool broad, which makes for stronger horses for the future.

While certainly not in danger of disappearing, the Ranger isn't nearly as widely known as America's other spotted horse. But that doesn't mean that owners of "the Using Horse of the High Plains" are any less enthusiastic. Making a devoted following, there are plenty of riders who are at home on the Rangerbred.

THE FLORIDA CRACKER HORSE

**H**AVE SOME HORSES FOUND THE FOUNTAIN of youth, once searched for in vain by Spanish explorer, Ponce de León? Perhaps not, but the area this explorer investigated became home to the Florida Cracker Horse, a rare equine whose small numbers are continuously supported by a few devoted horse lovers.

Breed History

In the early 1500s, when Ponce de León arrived on American shores, he became the first in a string of individuals to bring horses and other livestock to the southern coast of Florida. These horses from the Iberian Peninsula carried the blood of the North African Barb, foundation horse for dozens of breeds around the world. The Sorraia (a near-extinct feral Spanish horse), the Jennet, (a now-extinct war horse), and the Andalusian also found their way into the gene pool of the horses that put their hooves on the shores of the Americas.

More than one hundred years later, cattlemen set up massive ranching operations in the South and around the Gulf of Mexico. Horse breeding also started to take a strong foothold. As was the case for many breeds, Spanish horses that had either been turned loose or had escaped gathered together to live in feral herds. With a genetic background similar to those of the Spanish Mustang, Paso Fino, Peruvian Paso, and Criollo, the feral horse that would later become the Cracker Horse thrived in the climate of humidity, heat, and often changeable tropical weather. Over decades, natural selection helped hone the horses into intelligent, quick, agile, and hardy animals.

❶ver decades, natural selection helped the Florida Cracker Horse develop into an equine with intelligence, stamina, agility, and maneuverability.

Although small in stature, the sturdy Cracker Horse can easily carry adults.

Some of these small, crafty horses were captured by Native Americans who began to train them for their own use. Later, white settlers also began to integrate the feral Spanish-blooded horses into their breeding programs. The results were fantastic: they created horses with excellent cow sense, able to work long days in the humid Florida climate. When not herding cattle, they doubled as buggy horses and family horses, too. But they proved their mettle time and again as a ranch horse. They came to be known as Cracker Horses, named for the way cattlemen rounded up the cunning Spanish cattle by way of snapping loud bull-whips, making a "cracking" sound. Yet Cracker Horses have been known by a variety of names, depending on who was working them, including the Chickasaw Pony, Seminole Pony, Marsh Tackie, Prairie Pony, Florida Horse, Florida Cow Pony, and even Grass Gut.

Together with the Cracker Horse, farmers were able to tame the wilds of Florida and turn it into an area with a tremendous agricultural future.

Still, their numbers did not skyrocket like the more common cow horses, such as the American Quarter Horse. In fact, it was actually the rise of the American Quarter Horses that contributed to the Cracker Horse's dwindling favor.

After the Great Depression in the 1930s, many farmers moved their ranch operations from the Dust Bowl region of America to the more fertile regions of Florida. Unwittingly, they brought with them a parasite, the screw worm, which threatened the ranching industry in the state. Prior to the screw worm infestation, all a cowboy needed was a good Cracker horse to herd and pen the cattle, but screw worm parasites meant veterinary treatment. Now cattle didn't just need herding, they needed to be roped and held fast while medication was administered. Larger, sturdier horses were needed: the Quarter Horse stepped in. The services of the Cracker Horse were no longer required.

This could have spelled the end for the Cracker Horse, if not for a handful of concerned farmers who continued to breed them, instead of crossing them to other breeds and losing their purity forever. These farmers, including Ayers, Harvey, Bronson, Partin, Matchetts, and Whaley, maintained what would become the foundation stock of the breed. The early 1980s saw breed enthusiasts working with the Florida State Department of Agriculture to donate horses for the purpose of setting up herds in the Withlacoochee State Forest and the Paynes Prairie State Preserve. In 1989, The Florida Cracker Horse Association was set up as a nonprofit, volunteer-run organization. The next year, guidelines were established to determine which horses would be registered, and in 1991 the organization began registering Florida Cracker horses based on their history and conformation. Because the registry was so strict with its requirements, Crackers remain a consistent breed. Today, the Florida Cracker's numbers continue their slow upward growth. In 1997, only a few more than a hundred

COMPARABLE BREED

Sharing a similar genetic base, the Peruvian Paso, a Latin gaited breed bred by Peruvian plantation owners in the 1700 and 1800s, was created to carry riders comfortably over long distances with its unique gaits. It has a small, compact frame and when it exhibits its trademark gaits of the paso llano, sobreandando, *and* huachano, *the hooves travel out to the side, what breed aficionados call "termino." The breed is shown at gaited and breed shows, and makes an excellent trail horse.*

horses were registered, but enthusiasts, banking on the breed's importance to Florida's heritage, are hopeful that breeders and owners can raise this number to 750 by the year 2005.

Breed Characteristics

The Cracker Horse is small yet sturdy, standing about 13.5 to 15 hands high, weighing in at around 800 to 950 pounds. It often has a slightly dished profile to its small head, with wide-set eyes, and ears in proportion to the face. The neck is of medium length, well-defined, fairly narrow, and not cresty, springing out of a nicely sloping shoulder. The horse's sturdy back is on the short side and its body is narrow, but with well-sprung ribs. The croup is sloping and short, and the tail is set moderately low.

The Cracker is not generally considered a gaited horse, although some Crackers possess a couple of their own unique gaits, being able to perform a type of running walk, which is a naturally fast walk, and a single-foot gait which, in true southern Cracker circles, is often called a "coon rack." The Cracker Horse can be found in all colors of the horse spectrum, but bays, browns, roans, and grays are most common. They are known for their amazing agility and stamina, their herding instinct, swiftness, and their unusual fast walking gait.

Lovers of the little Florida Cracker know that the best way to get hooked on one is to swing a leg over its back. Once comfortably in the saddle, a rider will discover how easy their gaits are to sit, and how much ground the pint-sized horse can cover. The Cracker Horse is enthusiastic about taking its charges wherever they want to go. Although their numbers are small, the horse itself is enormous in spirit and willingness.

THE MINIATURE HORSE

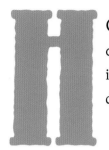**OW CUTE TINY THINGS ARE!** From model trains to little collections of dolls, Americans are fascinated with all things small. If it comes in a regular size, you can bet someone wanted to shrink it down to toy dimensions. Horses are no exception.

Breed History

The American Miniature Horse's ancestors come from many different breeds, spanning several hundred years. From English and Dutch mining horses, brought to America in the 1800s for use in the Appalachian coal mines, to British Shetland Ponies, to the tiny Argentinean Falabella, the Miniature Horse's original foundation stock comes from all over the world. Over the centuries, tiny horses were often found in royal stables, and have been thought of as a sign of wealth and extravagance. European aristocracy provided their children with these uncommon miniatures to play with. In the simplest terms, the Miniature Horse is the lovable result of breeding for size—and making sure not to "super-size it".

In the early 1900s, when horses turned from utilitarian to recreational in America, the idea of keeping horses as pets began to gain a foothold. As decades passed, American breeders, who had used a good deal of Shetland Pony blood, imported miniatures from other countries to improve the gene pool. No longer merely a symbol of extravagance and wealth, by the mid 1970s, everyday people were able to afford these small prizes.

Breeders of Miniatures seek to produce a small, sound, well-balanced horse that has the same good conformation found in regular-sized breeds.

In 1978, enthusiasts of the Mini established a registry for their diminutive charges. The American Miniature Horse Association (AMHA) was formed in order to help register, evaluate, and uphold the quality breeding of minis.

Miniatures are ideal for adults who want equine companionship yet don't want to ride. Driving events are especially popular.

COMPARABLE BREED

The Falabella, from Argentina, is a rare tiny horse that was bred by the Falabella family just before the turn of the twentieth century. Selecting smaller and smaller horses from the English Thoroughbred, the Shetland Pony and the South American Criollo, the resulting tiny horses were not ponies, but horses in miniature standing no more than 33 inches at the shoulder. They are used for driving and as companion animals.

Breed Characteristics

Miniature Horses are different from ponies. They are proportioned just like a horse, so they don't have the short cannons, the larger heads or other traits of ponies. The Mini has only one distinct requirement in order to be registered. It must be no taller than 34 inches at the withers. Other than that, the horse can be any color, and any type of conformation. Prior to 1987, a suitably tiny horse of any breeding was eligible for registration with the American Miniature Horse Association. Since then, however, only offspring of AMHA-registered sires and dams are allowed.

People love their Minis not just as pets, either. They are excellent first-time horses for those who don't want to ride. Because of their size, they really shouldn't be ridden and, if they are, then only by the tiniest of children, yet they still can introduce kids to the wonders and responsibilities of equines without the inherent complications of big horses. And even though they are rarely found under saddle, Minis make great show horses. They are usually shown in hand, or in harness, driven in pairs or in single hitch. They can even be shown in jumping classes, where a handler will jog the horse over a set of fences.

For those who love their small charges and big competition, the AMHA National Show, held every fall, is the place where tiny champions are crowned.

More than one thousand horses from around the nation come together each year to compete in a host of different events. The venue changes every year, rotating between Fort Worth, Texas; Lexington, Virginia; and Reno, Nevada. For competitors who love traveling, this gives them the opportunity to see different parts of the country. The venue change also assists the infrequent competitor who might only be able to afford to show when the competition is nearby.

Classes such as halter, various driving events, hunter and jumper classes, obstacle courses, showmanship, costume, and liberty (the only class where the horse is not shown in hand) make up the bulk of the competition.

Miniatures make great companions for people who may not be able to handle a full-sized horse, such as those who are older or disabled. They have proven to be excellent horses in therapeutic programs. And there is even a group of people who are training Miniature Horses to act as helpers for the sight-impaired—guide horses, if you will. It is important to remember that even though they are the size of large dogs, they still have the same instincts any prey animal is born with. So while they may seem like the right size for being helper horses, it still remains to be seen whether they can be desensitized 100 percent of the time to the hazards of urban life,

*M*ini mares and foals still need the same prenatal and postnatal care as regular horses

including traffic, people, and noise. Additionally, even though small, they are livestock and have completely different feeding, housing, and exercise requirements from dogs.

Miniature Horses can be affordable alternatives for people who've always wanted a horse, as they need less room to roam and less feed to eat. But they still need regular maintenance, just like any horse. That means routine hoof trimming (they usually don't require shoes), veterinary care, and the training required for those that are asked to perform. Their coats often grow in very thick and shaggy, so many owners perform full body clips on their tiny charges.

Interestingly enough, while many breeders are opting to create equines that are larger, stronger and faster, the Miniature Horse enthusiasts like to have their

Miniature Horses have their own pint-sized tack and equipment, right down to their transportation.

Miniatures are not ponies; they are horses that were selectively bred over decades to be tiny versions of their full-size counterparts.

fun scaled down. And while bigger might be better in some cases, Minis prove that being little can lead to greatness, too.

Famous Miniatures

Cuddles, the seeing-eye Mini, is one of the first horses to assist the disabled in a role where canines have generally dominated. In the late 1990s, this tiny equine made a media splash, hitting the streets wearing a seeing-eye harness and four small tennis shoes. Since Cuddles's debut, other helper horses have been enlisted to assist the sight-impaired.

THE MISSOURI FOX TROTTER

L IKE MANY AMERICAN BREEDS, born out of necessity and perhaps a little ingenuity, the Missouri Fox Trotter is a reflection of its breeders' desire to make work a pleasure. With its smooth-moving, distinctive gait, rugged good looks, and amiable attitude, the Fox Trotter is one of the older pleasure breeds in America.

Breed History

In the early 1800s, horse racing was a popular American pastime, and pleasure horses often doubled as racers on the weekends. In the foothills of the beautiful Ozarks, a breed of horse was just in its infancy. After the Louisiana Purchase, hundreds of new residents flooded south to Missouri, with its beautiful rolling green hillsides, rich forests, and plentiful water. The settlers began breeding the eastern-bred Morgans, Arabians, and Thoroughbreds they had brought with them to native stock, hoping to create the quintessential race and work horse. The resulting horses were honest, willing workers, able to toil in the field and pull the family buggy during the week, then switch over to being weekend racers and surefooted trail horses. They also had an interesting broken gait that made them easy to ride. Soon the settlers' horses were reflecting particular bloodlines that were in big demand, including the Brimmers, descended from Thoroughbred stock, and Jolly Roger and Old Skip, of Morgan/Thoroughbred origin.

But as the Deep South was and is known for its religious devotion, what was once a pastime—racing—was soon looked upon as "the devil's work", so it swiftly fell out of favor. Instead, breeders of the new Missouri horse decided that rather than speed, they'd emphasize their mount's way of going. Given fresh direction,

Developed from horses in the Ozarks, the breed, known by enthusiasts as "every rider's pleasure horse," is characterized by a gentle disposition.

The trademark gait of the Missouri Fox Trotter is performed when the horse is walking with the front legs while trotting with the hind legs.

breeding took on a whole new focus, and the horses chosen for breeding programs possessed a trademark broken gait that would easily and comfortably carry a rider over even the roughest of terrain. With an infusion of American Saddlebred blood, as well as that of the Standardbred (known for its ability to pace), and the Tennessee Walking Horse, the horse's stature grew, its conformation improved, and its distinctive gait refined itself into a fox trot.

The horse from the Ozark Mountains became the breed of choice for local doctors, sheriffs, postmen, and others wanting to make their rounds comfortably, and in style. Breeders looked to pass along that smooth-moving gait, but they also worked carefully to create a tractable, willing temperament in their pleasure horse, making him even more desirable as a leisure and workhorse.

In the middle of the next century, a group of horse breeders decided to put together an organization to help preserve the type of horse that had been so carefully bred in the Ozarks. Formed in 1948, The Missouri Fox Trotting Horse Breed Association began registering horses that met their standards, which were stamina, soundness, gentle disposition, and the unique fox-trotting gait. Unfortunately, many of the original records were lost forever in an office fire not long after its inception.

Ten years later, the association reemerged from the ashes, reorganized and ready to go. The registry accepted equines that met their requirements all the way up until 1982, when it closed the books. After that time, foals had to have both parents registered with the Missouri Fox Trotting Association to be accepted into the registry.

Because the Ozark area of Missouri had plentiful cattle ranches, Missouri Fox Trotters weren't as affected by the age of mechanization as other breeds. Ranchers continued to use them long after the turn of the century while other breeds' numbers dwindled dramatically. Cattle ranchers were not the only ones taken with the horse's gifts. In the coming decades, Fox Trotters would take on new roles as surefooted trail mounts, field competition horses, and endurance and pleasure companions.

Breed Description

The Missouri Fox Trotter is a compact, medium-sized horse, standing from about 14 hands to a limit of 16 hands high. It is close-coupled, with a short but well-proportioned back that has a broad, weight-bearing surface. Its well-sprung ribs create a solid barrel. Its sloped shoulder sits underneath slightly rounded withers, allowing the horse to execute the fox trot gait naturally. The legs are clean, with dense bone, and good muscling above the knee and hock. The feet, renowned for surefootedness, are tough as nails and the perfect size to capably support the horse's frame. From the withers, the powerfully built neck springs out at a slight angle, carrying an honest head with a straight profile, small ears, and expressive eyes. Sporting thick, full manes and tails, the breed is shown with its distinctive pair of braids woven in at the top of the bridle path. The horse can come in a

Missouri Fox Trotters are bred in a variety of coat colors.

variety of coat colors: including chestnut, cremello, champagne, palomino, black, bay, gray, and pinto-patterned.

The fox trot is the horse's signature, a diagonal gait in which the horse is walking in the front and trotting in the back. As a result of its ideal conformation, the horse oversteps his front hoof prints with his hind prints, placing his back feet on the ground with a gliding action. Active and fairly ground-covering, the fox trot will carry the horse and rider smoothly at a rate of about eight to ten miles an hour. With both head and tail carried high, a fox-trotting horse is a picture of noble carriage and easy-striding animation. But that's not all: the horse also has an active, free-flowing walk, and gentle canter to complement its trademark gait.

Held every fall in Ava, Missouri, the Missouri Fox Trotting Horse World Show and Celebration is the pinnacle of fox-trotting success. From lead-line classes for the wee fox-trotting lovers, to the professional divisions, the Celebration is

The Fox Trotter's gait is a rhythmic one. In the show ring or in exhibitions, ribbons braided into the mane fly as the head, ears, and tail nod to the beat.

COMPARABLE BREED

Puerto Rico's Paso Fino ("fine step" in Spanish), is famous for its four-beat lateral gait, which is remarkably easy to sit. The movements of the horse are absorbed in its back and croup, giving the rider a smooth ride. Smaller than the Fox Trotter, he has brio, or "hidden fire", coupled with a pleasing temperament.

designed to showcase the horse's talents. Other classes include sidesaddle, equitation, English pleasure, and western pleasure. Additionally, the Versatility arena classes highlight athleticism, as horses perform in reining, stake races, pole bending, barrel racing, and water glass classes, in which riders must hold a full glass of water while performing at various gaits without spilling a drop.

And while the breed association's year-end events showcase the Missouri Fox Trotter as a competition mount, its aficionados understand that each pleasure horse is also a winner. Folks enamored with the Fox Trotter's gifts enjoy letting others know what their horses mean to them. And their home state appreciates the breed's gifts so much that the Fox Trotter is Missouri's official state horse. Whether in competition or just taking its owner across those uneven trails with never a bad step, the Fox Trotter easily dances its way into its rider's hearts.

Famous Missouri Fox Trotters

Old Skip, a prepotent sire in the Missouri Fox Trotter breed, featured some Morgan and Thoroughbred blood. Old Skip's lineage can be found in many champion Fox Trotters.

The Rockaway line of Missouri Fox Trotters was also found under the name of Black Squirrel horses. The Black Squirrel pedigree was the foundation of many early Fox Trotters. Two of the most famous, **Golden Governor** and **Chester Dare,** came from foundation Black Squirrel horses.

THE MORAB

WHEN WORLDS COLLIDE—the making of the Morab was just that. Taking one history from centuries ago and on the other side of the world, and combining it with America's not too distant past has resulted in a horse that fans say is the perfect blend to fulfill their needs.

The Morab, as its name suggests, is a combination of Morgan and Arabian blood. The Arabian, nurtured for centuries by the Bedouin tribes of the Middle East, and the Morgan, a product of mysterious breeding which nevertheless made a great impact on Colonial America and beyond, provide the ingredients for success.

Morgan enthusiasts are quite vocal in their love for their breed, but then, so are Arabian lovers. Today, their equally devoted admirers have found that when the two come together, the result is an attractive and talented horse.

Breed History

Although the Morab is certainly not an ancient breed in itself, the Arabian dates back many centuries, and the Morgan is nearly as old as America. But to give the breed an actual starting point, you'd probably have to go back just to the mid-nineteenth century. Golddust, a palomino stallion born in 1855, was the offspring of a Morgan stallion and an Arabian mare. He turned out to be a magnificent show horse in saddleseat classes, dazzling spectators with his presence and his flashy way of going. He was also quite a speed demon, winning handily at the racetrack in harness trotting events. He sealed his place in history, however, by being prepotent at stud. He, like his ancestor Justin Morgan, was

The Morab often displays a dished profile, reflecting its Arabian ancestry.

able to impart his characteristics to a new generation of colts and fillies. Soon, many Americans were seeking out this horse that could produce quick, graceful carriage horses.

In the 1920s, millionaire publishing mogul William Randolph Hearst began breeding horses for his expansive cattle operation in central California. He decided that a Morgan/Arabian cross would be ideal for his purposes—they were handy around cattle, and attractive on top of that. Hearst even gave the breed its Morab name, and soon after, other ranchers followed suit, appreciating the horse's stamina, ability to work long days, and sensibility under saddle and on the ground.

Later, the breed took a different turn. In the 1950s Martha Doyle Fuller, a Morab breeder, decided that while the ranch life was one outlet for the horse's talents, the true calling for the horse was in the show arena. She began to selectively breed Morabs for type and flashiness. Her daughter took her work one step further, and founded the first Morab breed registry in 1973.

"The best of both worlds," say Morab lovers, combining the strength, eagerness, and agility of the Morgan with the stamina, beauty, and intelligence of the Arabian.

COMPARABLE BREED

The French Anglo-Arab is a common saddle horse. While Anglo-Arabs, which are basically a cross between an English Thoroughbred and an Arabian, are found all over the world, the French type is very distinct. And like the Morab, breeding Anglo-Arabs to Anglo-Arabs has resulted in more refined horses. These light horses are generally about 16 hands tall and are used in pleasure and in competition.

Now there are two permanent breed registries that serve the Morab: the North American Morab Horse Association and the International Morab Breeder's Association.

Breed Characteristics

The Morgan and the Arabian are similar in some aspects, particularly modern Morgans. Both are beautiful, with fine features and proud carriage. From the Arabian, the Morab gets an extra boost of endurance, stamina, and grace; from the Morgan side, the horse gets strength, power, and agility. The result is a horse that doesn't contradict—it simply complements itself.

The Morab stands about 15 hands in height and is well muscled, yet still remains refined. It may have a straight or slightly concave profile to its smallish head. It has prominent nostrils to take substantial amounts of air into its large-capacity lungs. It has wide-set, intelligent eyes, small, alert ears, and a beautifully curved neck. The short back, powerful haunches, clean legs with dense bone and strong, well-formed hooves all lend to it being a sound horse.

The Morab is not just a cross of two different horses. Farms that mate Morab to Morab in second- and third- generation breedings know that theirs is an actual type, so much so that they can predict what type of Morab they will create. This goes a long way to dispel some of the criticism that the Morab is not a real breed.

While some might think that the Morab is a part-bred or merely a cross between Arabians and Morgans, it has come to be known as a distinct breed.

To further this, both breed registries require their horses have documented Arabian and Morgan pedigrees, and that the resulting foal be no more than 75 percent of either foundation breed. So a horse that is 90 percent Arabian and 10 percent Morgan, for example, is not considered a Morab.

With a history of being used for working cattle, the Morab is not just another pretty face. Morgan blood tames some of the hotter Arabian blood, making for a horse that accepts training and guidance well. A good all-around horse, certainly, but there are some disciplines in which Morab lovers find their horses excel. As show horses, Morabs have the animation and beauty that many riders in saddleseat classes such as English country pleasure look for. In a different area altogether are the wild and wooly endurance riders, a seat-of-the-pants group that likes their horses fast, sound, and controllable. They are now finding that Morabs are a great option compared with their purebred Arabian cousins. And in yet a different venue from the great outdoors of endurance and competitive trail is the elegant realm of dressage, where collection, throughness, obedience, forwardness, and brilliance are the key to success, and often the Morab knows how to unlock those doors. Their naturally uphill carriage, and their beautiful swinging gaits that flow easily from extension to collection, are earning high marks on dressage tests.

Besides having several state and regional shows, the U.S. Morab Nationals/ The United Classic are the crowning glory, taking place every October at the Illinois State Fairgrounds in Springfield. This is a USA Equestrian A-rated show for Morgans, Arabians, and Half Arabians. There are futurities for fillies and colts, championship classes for stallions, mares, and geldings, pleasure classes (country, hunter, and western), and liberty classes, where the horses are shown without handlers. There is a "Champagne Evening" where the Morab halter and futurity classes are held as an elegant affair at night.

Morab enthusiasts say that, above all, those who are drawn to the breed love it for its affectionate nature, and its need to bond with its owner. The horse truly appreciates human companionship, and they desire to please their handlers. It seems that this too, has been passed along in the horse's very different histories. From the desert Arabian, beloved by its Arabic caretakers to the point where poetry written about them has been handed down through the ages, to America's little powerhouse, outperforming horses twice its size or breeding, the Morab bridges these two great histories, and can now create its own.

THE MORGAN

AMERICA LOVES TALL TALES AND FOLKLORE. Look at the story of Paul Bunyan and his famous pal Babe, the giant blue ox. Or Johnny Appleseed, planting apple trees throughout the nation. For Americans, there's nothing better than stories about larger-than-life characters, or the little guy triumphing over adversity—our own versions of David and Goliath. There is a breed of horse whose history is laced with so much legend it almost borders on fiction but, for the most part, it's true.

The Morgan is considered to be the first documented native breed in America, and can be traced back to one stocky little stallion with the strength of a draft horse and the speed of a Thoroughbred. Today's Morgans, like their foundation stallion, have the ability to excel in a number of equestrian disciplines. They have the appeal of both a show horse and a family horse, and a kind temperament to handle both roles with aplomb.

Breed History

In the late eighteenth century, New England farmers were known for keeping only one horse, and needing him to "do it all." The workhorse during the week doubled as the weekend driving horse, hitched to smartly take the family into town. Legendary, however, were the match races and contests of strength in which these horses also participated.

A logging horse named Figure was born in West Springfield, Massachusetts in 1789 of unknown parentage. While some historians name True Briton, an English Thoroughbred, as the colt's sire, others point to possible Canadian

Hailing from Vermont, the blood of foundation stallion Justin Morgan can be found in every modern Morgan horse.

The Morgan's flashy way of going makes it suited to fine-harness driving.

Horse, Welsh Cob, Friesian, or even Norfolk Trotter within his genetic mix. When Figure was a yearling he was given to a schoolteacher named Justin Morgan as payment for a debt. Morgan decided to get the most out of the young horse, and Figure was loaned out to neighboring farms, where he toiled as a plow and logging horse. The horse was compact and close-coupled in build, but with clean legs, and beautiful knee action. He also had powerful hindquarters, and a broad chest that gave him ample breathing capacity.

As the little stallion matured, it was soon discovered that he could outrun the fastest Thoroughbreds in match races. The teacher was, like his townspeople, always game to pit his little horse—standing only about 14 hands—against other horses in competition. They'd go head to head in speed races, have log-pulling contests (where Figure would beat the massive draft horses in pulling heavy loads), or even trotting races on country roads. Villagers would make the pulling contests even tougher by sitting astride the large load, but Figure could easily haul the weight.

Figure's most notable race was in 1796, when he competed against two Thoroughbreds. But he didn't race them together—he ran against each one consecutively. The rough country course did nothing to stop Figure, but it proved to be a challenge for the Thoroughbreds. The little horse not only kept up with the long-legged racers, he pulled away from both, showing them a clean pair of heels.

As Figure's legend grew in Vermont, farmers began asking for the little stallion's stud services. Local mares of various breeding, including English Thoroughbred and Norfolk Trotter, made up a good portion of his roster. He was very prepotent, passing along his similar conformation and aptitude. The stallion put his stamp on future generations, re-creating his own likeness with amazing success. Figure began being referred to as Morgan's horse, and then took on the name of his owner.

Even after Justin Morgan—the horse—passed on, his legacy was only beginning. By the mid-1800s, offspring of Justin Morgan were considered as a true type of horse. The Morgan became known for its snappy action in harness, and its famous trotting ability made it a favorite harness racing horse during the 1840s. In 1845, one of Figure's great-granddaughters, Fanny Jenks, trotted one hundred miles in 9 hours, 38 minutes and 34 seconds, pulling a regular wagon, not a driving sulky. On the track, a great-grandson, Ethan Allen, set a new record for trotting one mile, and was victorious in several other trotting races. He was only defeated once—by his own son.

As tastes changed in racing, proper long-distance courses and stayers replaced earlier country sprints. Harness racing also took on a more serious, competitive nature, and an emerging breed, the Standardbred, was being crafted to burn up the tracks. Even though the role for the racing Morgan was coming to an end, its blood was used to help refine the Standardbred as a blazing-fast trotting horse.

Morgans served as cavalry mounts during the American Civil War—on both sides. They also helped deliver the mail via the Pony Express in the late 1800s. In

While many Morgans sport dark coats like Justin Morgan's, there are several other possible coat colors.

1894, the first volume of the American Morgan Horse Register was opened. A few years later, in 1909, the Morgan Horse Club was formed to support the Morgan breed and the breeder's efforts.

After the turn of the century, with mechanization and the rise of sport horses that were more specialized, the Morgan's numbers began to dwindle. There were several years when Morgan breeders produced fewer than one hundred foals. The US Department of Agriculture, coupled with the efforts of concerned breeders, helped bring the breed's numbers back to very healthy levels. In 1948, in an effort to preserve the characteristics of the breed, the studbook was closed to all horses that did not have registered Morgan parentage. More than 132,000 animals have since been registered. The Morgan Horse Club continued to change and adapt with the breed's ongoing needs and in 1971 underwent reorganization and was renamed The American Morgan Horse Association.

The typical stance of a Morgan shown in hand is the "parked-out" stretch to best exhibit the horse's conformation.

COMPARABLE BREED

The Friesian, a riding and carriage horse from Holland, is sometimes considered a draft horse because of its conformation, but its size and breeding put it actually in the warmblood category. Standing at about 15 hands in height, the Friesian's compelling beauty and natural high-stepping way of going is similar to that of the Morgan. Like the Morgan, the Friesian has found many enthusiasts in the world of dressage calling upon its talents.

Morgan registry may be exclusive now, but in previous years, it was the Morgan that influenced several other American breeds, including the Standardbred, Tennessee Walking Horse, and American Quarter Horse. Nearly 90 percent of today's American Saddlebreds have Morgan blood.

Breed Characteristics

The Morgan is a compact horse, with a lovely expressive face, large, intelligent eyes, and a straight or slightly dished profile. The slightly crested neck blends into well-defined withers. The Morgan is known as being a sound horse with flat bone and good substance to its limbs, yet he is refined, almost delicate in appearance. But don't let his beauty fool you. This horse is a powerhouse, with a short back, sturdy legs, and good well-muscled haunches.

Today's Morgans are a little taller than the foundation stallion, standing anywhere from 14.1 to 15.2 hands. Morgans have developed into two basic types: the old-style Morgan, which is stout and powerful, and the modern Morgan, an elegant, refined park horse. Both are known for having excellent stamina and vitality as well as a good nature, which is one thing breeders never want to change.

Morgans are usually bay, black, or dark chestnut, but because of cross-breeding with a variety of different mares before the stud book was closed, there

are modern Morgans in a variety of hues, including palomino and buckskin. There should not be excessive white on the Morgan, however.

Friends of the Morgan often disagree over the two types within the breed. Some believe that all Morgans should reflect the foundation sire—as the powerful, old-style Morgan does. Others prefer to see the breed excel as a showy, high-stepping park horse, with the refinement and carriage seen in breeds such as Arabians and American Saddlebreds. Several groups have formed as a result, each promoting the talents of their particular Morgan type.

With versatility and performance continuing to define the breed, the Morgan's reputation is growing in sports such as combined driving and dressage. It was the first American breed to represent the USA in the World Pairs driving competition in 1997. More western riding enthusiasts are discovering the breed's talents, as Morgans delve into athletic events such as cutting and reining. Since many are small enough to be eligible for pony classes, they also make fine mounts for kids—and not just as a beginner's horse. For junior riders who want to be very competitive, the Morgan is an excellent choice.

Many breeds specialize in certain areas, and while Morgans are great all-around riding horses, they also are beautifully at home in harness. One reason is their classy, animated trot. In combined driving, horses compete in a series of events, similar to the way ridden horses do in combined training, otherwise known as horse trials or the three-day event. Combined driving demonstrates the horse's ability in driven dressage,

Morgan foals often display their trademark animated gaits and alertness from birth.

obstacle driving, which involves a course of cones, and a marathon cross-country phase over ten to sixteen kilometers, depending upon the event.

At Morgan breed shows, judges look for regular cadence, the ability to collect and extend the gait, and balanced action. But the other gaits are also just as important. A true three-beat canter, animated but smooth, and a regular working walk are the basics. The Grand National & World Championship Morgan Horse Show is held in October in Oklahoma City. The Oklahoma State Fairgrounds come alive with excitement as Morgans compete in a variety of classes including park horse classes, both driven and under saddle, pleasure driving, in-hand classes, English pleasure, and western pleasure.

Today's Morgan is seeing a faithful following growing amongst a sea of warmbloods: in the dressage arena. Its naturally uphill build, its active gaits, and responsive nature are perfect for the various movements of shoulder-in, half-pass, canter pirouette, and tempi changes. Perhaps these are unusual callings for a diminutive equine, but the Morgan is ready, willing, and able to compete head to head with Europe's finest. And that's the stuff future legends are made of.

Famous Morgans

Comanche, that famous brave horse who was said to be the only survivor at the Battle of Little Big Horn (also known as Custer's Last Stand), was thought to have been a Morgan.

Rienzi was the mount of Union General Philip Sheridan. Sheridan rode his horse during the Civil War to rally his troops. Rienzi also went by the name of Winchester, and both Sheridan and Winchester were commemorated in a poem and a painting, both titled *Sheridan's Ride* by Thomas Buchanan Read. Today, Civil War buffs can still see Rienzi's remains at the Smithsonian Museum.

The Morgan is often found in "park horse" classes where saddleseat is the norm.

THE MUSTANG

IT'S A SCENE STRAIGHT OUT OF an old-time Western. A band of horses picks its way slowly across the high desert, searching through the ravines for scrub grass or any sustenance. Heads lowered, tails whisking away flies, they busily forage as the sun continues its path into the sky. Suddenly, a head rises above the sea of sorrels, dark bays, and pintos, and ears are pricked forward. The herd, with stallion in the back and lead mare guiding the way, dashes off—but not in panic, for they know the routine. They make their way to a safer place, and then continue their quest for food. A symbol of the American West, the Mustang was built to endure. The Mustang has to be a survivor—its future lies in the hands of those who once tried to exterminate it: humankind.

Breed History

Many centuries ago, explorers and conquerors came to the Americas, bringing their horses with them. Native peoples saw these horses so prized by their masters and acquired their own through trade or theft.

A few escaped and began lives of freedom. They formed herds and lived without the hand of man to help them through the seasons. Those that survived winter to flourish the next spring went on to pass their genes to a new generation. Those that didn't became part of the natural selection process. As decades passed, these now-feral horses became more cunning, more hardy, and enduring. They were able to survive on vegetation with little nourishing value, and walk for miles to water. They became known as Mustangs, an Americanization of the Spanish word *mesteno*, which means "wild" or "ownerless". By the early nineteenth century they had expanded throughout the untamed West.

Once the horses are rounded up, the BLM determines which will be offered up for adoption and which will be returned to freedom.

When the BLM determines an overpopulation of Mustangs exists, the excess animals are rounded up, sometimes with the use of helicopters, and offered for adoption.

The West didn't remain virgin territory for long. American ranchers and settlers headed away from the Mississippi River, looking to start anew. In the process, there were casualties—forests, buffalo, Native Americans—nothing escaped the onslaught of settlers laying claim to these new territories. At the turn of the century, cattle ranching operations vied with Mustangs for grazing space on public lands. The West was no longer a frontier—it was settled, and the advent of the gas engine sealed the fate of many a working horse. And the wild horse? He was a liability—a nuisance for ranchers who leased public lands at a nominal fee from the government. The way to deal with the nuisance was to eliminate it just as the buffalo had been. So began the era of Mustang slaughter. Hundreds of thousands of horses were captured and shot, their bodies ground into pet food.

Ranchers often said, "Mustangs are no good—they're worth more in the can."

Not everyone felt that way, however. Throughout the 1950s, individuals tried to protest the mass destruction of these creatures. Velma Johnson, nicknamed "Wild Horse Annie" by her detractors, fought to get newspapers and television interested in the plight of wild horses. She also called upon the nation's youth to start a letter-writing campaign to Congress. These massive efforts by grade schoolers paid off. In 1959, the hunting of wild horses by airplane was banned.

In 1960, The International Society for the Protection of Mustangs and Burros was formed, to help create legislation to save the Mustang from being obliterated from the face of the earth. Animal welfare activists started getting the word out to the public about how wrong it was to destroy a creature that was thought of as a symbol of freedom. Soon the message reached the masses, and even those who were driving their Ford Mustangs became aware of this needless slaughter.

A few years later, in 1971, Congress passed the Wild Free-Roaming Horse and Burro act to stop the abuse and exploitation of the Mustang, stating that they were "living symbols of the historic and pioneer spirit of the West; they contribute to the diversity of life forms within the nation." The Bureau of Land Management was put in charge of protecting the horses and enforcing the law.

But all did not go smoothly for the bureaucratic organization. The law was supposed to prohibit Mustangs from being removed from public lands illegally; from being shot on public lands; from being exploited for commercial purposes; and from being taken by private parties without permission. But many of these activities were still taking place. Wild horses continued to be killed illegally, or shipped to slaughter.

In 1976, The BLM introduced its Adopt-A-Horse program, which allowed ordinary people to buy a real Mustang, fresh off the range, for a tiny fee. The

Because of the Wild Free-Roaming Horse and Burro Act of 1971, the Bureau of Land Management's primary responsibilities are to preserve and protect the Mustang and to ensure that they have healthy range to live on.

horse remained the property of the government for a year, and then full title was given to the adopter.

Most were eager to own their own spirited piece of history. And while each horse came with its own set of unique challenges, success stories were frequent.

One mistake the BLM made was eliminating the adoption fee. The argument for doing so was that the Mustang's numbers had swelled to an unmanageable size. At that point, about thirty thousand animals were given away for free and, sadly, many ended up going straight to slaughter. The BLM was ordered by a federal judge to reinstate the adoption fee in 1988 to prevent more horses from being killed.

There have been other troubles with the BLM's Mustang management over the years. The BLM has historically bowed to pressure from ranchers, who graze more than four million cattle on public lands. The areas that Mustangs have to live in are dwindling, and the BLM has claimed that there are an ever-increasing number of excess horses. Range conditions have not improved, and the number of horses pulled into the Adopt-A-Horse program has hit its limit. The media's sensationalistic portrayal of Mustangs as overpopulated and starving has also given the Mustang a renewed challenge to its survival in the wild.

Animal welfare organizations, with their increasing strength and ability to inform the media, continue to be watchdogs for the treatment of Mustangs. The BLM continues to work to improve conditions for the horses. Mustang associations are striving to increase awareness and education for adopters, as well as to keep the plight of the horse alive.

Adopting a Mustang

It's a sad fact that fewer Mustangs will be allowed to roam free in the years to come. Adoption will be the only means of finding Mustangs a new life in the private sector. At various locations around the

Although Mustangs are wild horses, they are the descendants of once-domesticated horses that were released or escaped onto public lands.

COMPARABLE BREED

Like the Mustang, the Brumby of Australia is a feral horse descended from domestic stock. It does not enjoy the protections that its American cousin does, however. Many are shot by the government from helicopters because of the impact feral animals have on the environment.

United States—and even online—ordinary people who meet the very easy criteria can take home a Mustang. Mustangs are an even greater responsibility than domestic horses yet, ironically, they are so much easier, and cheaper, to obtain. Adopters need only to be eighteen years of age and to sign a contract stating that they have adequate facilities and financial means to care for the animal. However, they're not required to have trained a horse before, or even to have ridden a horse in their lives!

Mustangs can be very shy, as all the blood in their veins tells them that man is predator. It takes a good understanding of equine behavior to get the horse to understand that people are their new herd leaders and not part of the mountain lion/coyote group.

Mustangs have survived on poor quality rations and shouldn't be given rich foods. Their hooves are flinty and tough, but still need regular maintenance just as those of any domestic horse, now that their natural way of wearing them down—miles of walking—has been taken away.

Mustangs don't need to be broken in the way of the old Westerns. Intelligent and often curious, they respond best to training done with respect. Problems encountered can often be solved with an understanding of equine communication and body language, not force. These horses are the epitome of a herd creature, so handlers must become the herd leader, the substitute for all other horses. Gaining the horse's confidence, piquing his curiosity, and giving him the opportunity to respond to the right training often wins him over.

For the successful pairings, there are plenty of options besides just pleasure riding. The National Wild Horse and Burro Show, held annually at the Reno, Nevada, Livestock Event Center at the beginning of summer, allows owners to show that their horses can do many things. The show helps promote the adoption of wild horses and burros and also helps participants and the public understand the need for gentle training techniques, proper nutrition, and adequate veterinary care for adopted horses and burros. The show's proceeds are used to support the next year's event as well as a grant program for range improvements within wild horse herd areas. A Mustang and burro auction is held at the show each year in conjunction with the competition.

The western division includes classes for halter, showmanship, trail, team penning, reining, western pleasure, and western riding. On the English side, classes include hunter hack, hunter under saddle, English pleasure, and pleasure driving. There are also speed events and games, such as keyhole and barrel racing, to test the mettle of both horse and handler.

Breed Characteristics

While most of us think of rippling coats and long waving manes and tails when we think of Mustangs, that is not always an accurate picture. Because Mother Nature can be harsh, the Mustang over the centuries has adapted to its environment. The resulting horses may not always be the prettiest creatures on hoof. They are usually pony-sized, although some can be up to 15 hands. They are of various shapes and sizes, but can be short in the neck, short in the leg, and large in the head. Their coats are often scarred from life in inhospitable conditions, although they can be found in all colors and patterns. For lovers of the Mustang, however, they are the noblest and most beautiful of creatures, personifying freedom.

Kiger

In the 1970s, the BLM found a small herd of Mustangs tucked away in the Oregon foothills. It was apparent that these horses had unique bloodlines: Spanish influences could be seen in their upright carriage, arched necks, wide-set eyes, curved ears, and stocky, muscular conformation. The herd was relocated to Steens

Mountain, and, in isolation, began to increase in number. While all Mustangs are presumed to have Spanish blood, most have been diluted through the centuries to some degree. But in the Kiger Mustang, the blood is much more pure.

The Kiger is often seen in the dun category, with horses that are dun, red dun, grulla, claybank, and even black in their midst. These horses often exhibit wild colorations, such as tiger stripes on forelegs and around hocks, as well as dorsal stripes.

The BLM realized that this was a special herd, and with help from an Oregonian enthusiast named Rick Littleton, the Kigers are receiving special attention. Their popularity continues to grow, and they are quite sought after, yet are rounded up only once every three to four years. Ranchers cannot destroy or move them from their protected habitat. Littleton and his wife began the Kiger Mustang Ranch, and established Steens Mountain Kiger Registry for the horses that come from the Steens Mountain herd.

Mustangs, once tamed, can perform in a variety of activities. Their natural intelligence and quickness make them ideal for ranch work.

While Mustangs may not have the completely free life that they once did, roaming free with ample forage and water, it is they that have now captured us: our imagination and our hearts.

Famous Mustangs

JB Andrew, a 16.3-hand black wild Mustang, was captured, trained, and became a successful competitor in the upper levels of dressage in the 1990s. JB, which stands for JailBird, became an ambassador for the Mustang and was so well liked that Breyer chose to make a model in his likeness.

Mustang Lady was a BLM Mustang who competed in the tough sport of endurance competitions and came in second in 1990 in the grueling Tevis Cup, a one-hundred-mile endurance race held in California. Lady also received three bronze medals in international competitions of one-hundred-mile rides.

Cloud, a cream-colored stallion whose life was documented in the 2001 PBS special and book, *Cloud, Wild Stallion of the Rockies,* introduced a new audience to the real life of a Mustang. The beautifully filmed documentary followed the horse from birth to five years of age. Breyer models commemorated the stallion that same year.

Nevada Joe Sterling, a dark bay gelding, became a crowd favorite in 2002 while traveling with famous clinician and trainer Pat Parelli. Nevada Joe's transformation from completely untrained Mustang to confident saddle horse was documented in the magazine *Horse Illustrated* over a twelve-month period. Parelli used him in front of crowds of thousands to show the trainability of Mustangs and the effectiveness of his Natural Horse*Man*Ship methods. Nevada Joe, too, was chosen by Breyer as a model horse.

THE NATIONAL SHOW HORSE

SOME HORSES ARE PERFECT PARTNERS in leisure, while others are great workmates. Then there are those whose calling is naturally in the "performing arts." In the case of the National Show Horse, his name says it all; this breed was created for competition from day one.

Taking two breeds with extraordinary show qualities in their own right, the Arabian and the American Saddlebred, several breeders joined together to devise a show horse unto its own.

From the Arabian came class, beauty, stamina, and expression. The Saddlebred contributed brilliance, animation, flash, and grace. To many, combining these two breeds seemed like a natural progression, blending the best of both worlds.

In the short time that the breed has existed, The National Show Horse has gained a very steady following. Created a little more than two decades ago, the NSH answered the call of the show ring with a resounding "yes." Today, more than fifteen thousand horses are registered with the breed association.

Breed History

The National Show Horse began as a result of saddleseat riders wanting to be competitive in half-Arabian show classes. When Gene LaCroix, an Arabian breeder, began to truly take note of the winners of these classes, he determined that the Saddlebred-Arabian cross was coming out on top pretty consistently. In 1981, LaCroix, who always had an eye out for talented Saddlebreds, developed the National Show Horse Registry (NSHR). The registry admitted horses that

Nearly all coat colors are permitted for National Show Horses, and many in fact are pinto-patterned.

The National Show Horse was bred to be an affordable choice for half-Saddlebred classes.

carried the blood of Arabians and Saddlebreds, and developed bylaws and breed standards for the fledgling breed. It gave breeders guidance for refining their horses, slowly and systematically improving the cross until they came to their ideal show horse.

The blend of the two breeds became very popular in the half-Arabian classes, and even on the AHSA show circuit. Judges responded enthusiastically to the size, gaits, athleticism, and brilliance of the National Show Horse.

Easily trainable, some National Show Horses have the talent to become trick or stunt horses.

Breed Characteristics

Elegance on the hoof, the National Show Horse is a picture of grace and nobility. Standing 15 to 16 hands high, it has an attractive head and an arched neck set high on deep, sloping shoulders. It has well sprung ribs and proportionate back and loins. The croup is somewhat on the level side, the legs are long and clean and the cannon bones are short. And those lovely legs are designed to snap up and step out with activity and high action. So while the horse started out as a crossbred, after multiple generations of breeding for type, it now has distinctive characteristics all its own. Supporters say that to call their horse a mere half Arab sells the breed short, since it can be shown in its own breed shows as well as on the open circuit, exploring these avenues with tremendous success.

The horse became an affordable alternative for people who wanted to get into the prestigious saddleseat show ring, but couldn't keep up with the big-time trainers' fees. With a natural uphill carriage and fancy knee action, as well as active hocks that step well underneath the horse's body to propel it forward, the National Show Horse automatically had presence for the show ring. But they also had the trainability, intelligence, and affection prized by Arabian enthusiasts.

When breed registration first opened in 1982, it allowed a period of time during which a variety of horses could be considered foundation stock for the breed. However, the registry now has specific requirements as to which horses can be allowed to enter the registry. To register with the NSHR, a horse has to have a minimum of 25 percent Arabian blood. In order to be an NSHR nominated stallion (the owner has to nominate his or her horse, and the nomination must be approved by the board), the stud must be registered by the Arabian Horse Registry of America or the American Saddlebred Horse Association, the NSHR, or approved by the board of directors.

Foals have to be sired by an NSHR-nominated sire. Breeders are able to use three types of mares: Arabians, Saddlebreds, or other National Show Horses, bred to a "nominated sire." So while a National Show Horse may occasionally be only one-quarter Arabian, or he may be nearly all Arabian, most NSHs are actually an

Like the Saddlebred, the National Show Horse performs the slow gait and rack, both of which can come quite naturally to the horse.

COMPARABLE BREED

The Hackney is a fine harness horse that has its roots in Great Britain. At one time, Hackneys were popular for pulling carriages in everyday life. This refined, elegant little horse possesses brilliant action similar to the National Show Horse, and also is considered a park horse. The Hackney Pony shares the studbook of the Hackney Horse. Both have high-stepping animation, alert, refined appearance, and uphill conformation.

equal mix of both. And while it may seem complicated, a breeder's ultimate goal is to create an affordable horse that has the qualities of the classic English pleasure horse for saddleseat, driving, English pleasure, equitation, and in-hand classes.

This doesn't mean that the NSH is relegated to only these activities. The dressage ring is another place where the horse is being seen, since their foundation breeds are quite successful performing the intricate requirements of classical riding. And when a show career is over, the horses are still cherished for their pleasure-riding capabilities.

The National Show Horse Registry really does emphasize "show". And the registry, being new, loves to usher in newcomers to the show world. The rules and classes are geared toward what is best for the horse, including their shoeing requirements, equipment allowances, and their competition bylaws.

Making it comfortable and pleasurable is what showing a National Show Horse is all about. The organization developed its show series so that participants could qualify for its year-end championships, and even offered prize money for riders, using a good chunk of its annual registration fees for the next year's awards. This is pretty unique in the horse world, as is the fact that membership

The ideal National Show Horse has the beauty and refinement of the Arabian, with the presence and general conformation of the Saddlebred.

dues are paid only once, instead of renewed annually. This program became so successful that Saddlebred and Arabian registries changed their membership dues policies to mirror that of the National Show Horse Registry.

The breed's shows have an air of excitement and enthusiasm that comes from both the horses and their fans. Classes demonstrate the horse in all gaits, and, thanks to their Saddlebred blood, NSHs also compete at the slow gait and the rack, which are four-beat gaits with extreme action. While these gaits are animated, they are also smooth and exhilarating to ride—and the rider doesn't have to post these gaits as would be necessary at the trot. The horse also has to perform at the walk, trot, and canter. Undoubtedly, it's the classes that feature the horse racking that get the most response, since people love to see an arena of horses flying around the arena, heads high, tails streaming, all the while keeping that four-footfall beat.

But even with all the show accolades, the fans of the breed say that they love their horses because of their kind, affectionate nature and their intelligence, things that we'd find in our best equine partners. Show horses, sure. But a friend who wants to please—that's a blue-ribbon equine.

Famous National Show Horses

Cisco Kid SF is a champion stallion with the NHSR and was one of the top sires in the breed in the late 1990s.

DC Magic, a National Show Horse broodmare, was a multi-champion in English, driving, and was undefeated in Native Costume during her show days in the 1990s. Her offspring are also champions within the breed.

THE PALOMINO

WHEN GOOD THINGS COME IN GILDED pretty packages, the gift is even more enchanting. That's why horse breeders often look to create fine specimens in exciting colors. While nature alone provides the alchemy that keeps us all in suspense until a foal is born, horse breeders try to narrow the odds so that there is a greater chance to guide that foal's colorful future. A horse that is talented with beautiful conformation is quite a find, but if it has a gorgeous, unusual coat, it's the icing on the cake.

Of course, it's the horse and not the color that is important, but with the numerous colors that horses can bear, it's only natural that people have at least one that is near and dear to their heart. Palomino lovers staunchly agree, and seem to think that blondes really do have more fun. The fact that the horses are not easy to come by makes them even more special.

Breed History

The palomino is a color, and not a breed per se, but some of America's finest breeds include Palominos in their rosters. While golden horses have shown up in all parts of the world throughout history, when people think of blonde horses with flaxen manes and tails, it's hard not to think of them as an American hot property.

There are several theories as to how the actual name for the color originated. Some say that it has a Spanish derivation, because Palomino is a common surname in Spain. Others believe that the horse is named for a ranch owned by

The flaxen mane and tail of the Palomino make this horse a true blonde bombshell.

The Palomino's ideal hue is that of a newly minted gold coin.

a Palomino family that bred a herd of golden horses. Some suggest that the name is a version of *paloma,* Spanish for dove, while others say that the Palomino horse is named for a golden Spanish grape.

In any event, Palominos landed on the shores of the Americas with the Spanish explorers in the sixteenth century. Their horses, called Isabellas after their queen, became popular in Mexico and the Southwest.

Breed Characteristics

Even though the Palomino is found all over the world, the United States was the country to create registries for these golden horses. To be registered with the American Palomino Horse Registry, a horse must have a light mane and tail, and the eyes must be dark or hazel, never blue, and both the same color. Colors can vary from light to dark. Many of these horses are also registered with other organizations including the American Saddlebred, Morgan, American Quarter Horse, and others.

Famous Palominos

The media has been kind to Palominos, with several notable horses bearing their gifts of gold. Ironically, many made their debut in black and white. But no matter, even without Technicolor, these horses were standouts. Roy Roger's **Trigger** carried the singing cowboy to many an adventure. Dale Evans, Roy's partner in movies and in life, also rode a golden horse named **Buttercup.**

In the realm of comedy, few could forget the famous talking horse **Mr. Ed.** A wisecracking American Saddlebred with a creamy golden coat, Mr. Ed and his human pal Wilbur delighted television viewers for many seasons.

Nautical, formerly a golden cow horse, became a United States Equestrian Team champion show jumper, and the subject of the 1960 Disney film, *The Horse with the Flying Tail.* He competed internationally and helped win a team show-jumping gold medal in the 1959 Pan American Games.

Palominos make a striking riding partner no matter what the breed. Reining horses, shown with long flowing manes and tails, are crowd-pleasing favorites. Dressage horses bearing gilded coats stand out from their

Breeders, particularly American Quarter Horse breeders, have worked to produce beautiful and athletic golden horses.

dark-coated brethren. And parades? Matched palominos, often of Saddlebred or American Quarter Horse derivation, always draw cheers of appreciation from the crowds. And while the saying still stands that a good horse is never a bad color, when a good horse comes in the color you desire, it's like hitting the golden jackpot.

Although the Palomino is a color breed, most can be found performing in western events.

PONY OF THE AMERICAS

MOST BREEDS' HISTORIES GO BACK FOR a hundred years or many more, but the Pony of the Americas is actually a relatively new creation, an ingenious pairing of two very different breeds that resulted in what many feel is the ideal mount for children. Considered the ultimate family pony, today's POA has captured the hearts of its enthusiasts, and is converting more equestrians to its spotted ranks each year.

Breed History

It was the early 1950s in Mason City, Iowa. A farmer who lived in an area dotted with horse ranches had a lovely Arabian/Appaloosa cross mare—very typey, with refined conformation, and colorful spotted coat. As things go in nature, one day the farmer found that his mare had been impregnated by a nearby Shetland Pony stallion. At that time, the farmer started to look for a new home for her. Enter Iowa attorney Les Boomhower, who bred Shetlands in addition to tending his thriving law practice. The farmer offered the mare to Boomhower, who at first turned him down. After all, who knows what the resulting foal would turn out like? Instead, he told the farmer that he'd wait until the foal was on the ground before he bought her.

Of course, the resulting foal was not an oddity. At the mare's side in the spring was a diminutive baby bearing wild Appaloosa markings—complete with what looked like a dark handprint on his hip. Seeing the colt, Boomhower immediately paid the farmer for both mare and foal and took them to his own farm.

The POA is small enough for little children to ride, yet still big enough for large kids and even some smaller adults to train.

The colt grew, but only to pony size. His beautifully colored coat set him apart from the other ponies that Boomhower was breeding. He had more substance than the Shetlands, but was still small and easy to handle. Boomhower called his pretty colt Black Hand, for his unusual markings. He had other breeders come look at him, and extolled the virtues of this youngster. Many agreed that this little crossbred would be the ideal kid's horse, able to compete in a variety of disciplines and be a solid equine citizen. But what to name this new creation? The group of breeders finally decided on Pony of the Americas, so called because it was the first pony type to originate in the USA. Black Hand became the foundation stallion for the breed, earning POA#1 in the new registry.

The registry established guidelines for their innovative pony. While many horses were bred with bloodlines similar to that of Black Hand, horses that didn't meet the registry requirements were not allowed to be POAs. Breeders wanted a horse small enough to be easily handled by children, yet it still had to

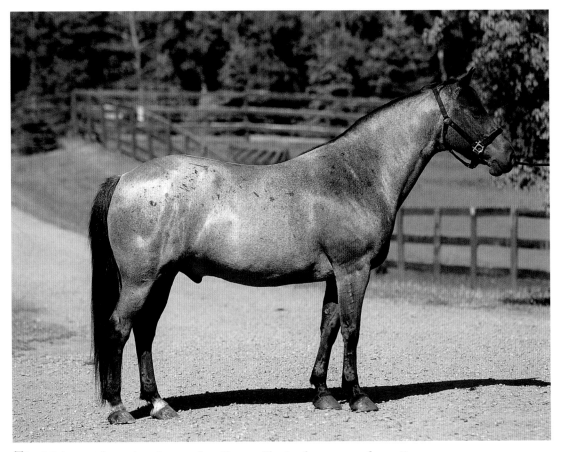

The POA must have Appaloosa coloration, with sturdy pony conformation.

COMPARABLE BREED

Most people think of ponies exclusively as kid's mounts, but the Welsh Pony, like the POA, has a devoted adult following, too. It can carry both children and small adults with ease. While broken down into four distinct categories of type, most have the physical characteristics of small, dished face with an alert profile, good legs, muscular bodies, and intelligence.

have Appaloosa color and versatility. Ponies could be no taller than 52 inches, and no smaller than 44 inches. Bearing the same profile as Black Hand, they had to have dished faces, a stocky build, and Appaloosa coloring. It was a challenge to get into the registry. Stringent show rules were set up right away as well. Because the breed was meant for children, if adults wanted to show them, they could only do so in hand, or in harness.

But from the beginning, an essential element that the pony had to have, no matter what, was color. While the Appaloosa Horse Club has solid Appaloosas competing in their breed shows, POA enthusiasts staunchly require that their horses bear spots in order to show in breed shows. And why not? A pint-sized pony with flashy markings is every young horse lover's dream. And although the breed registry allows crosses with several different breeds, including Appaloosas, Welsh, Connemara and Shetland Ponies, American Quarter Horses, Thoroughbreds, Morgans, and more, breeders have done well in keeping the gene pool full while retaining those lovely spotted patterns.

That's not to say that a solid POA is rejected from the fold completely. Solid-colored horses and ponies of unknown breeding can be registered as breeding stock if they pass an evaluation and are found to have no pinto coloring and no gaited stock in their ancestry. And nonregistered ponies that bear all the physical attributes of their registered brethren can gain regular entry into the club by being inspected for all physical characteristics of POAs.

POAs in Action

The new pony started to garner fans quickly, and as more were bred and registered, the need for the breed's own competitions sprung up. From local to state level, and finally a national show, POAs competed in all kinds of events, including gymkhana and western shows, driving and jumping competitions. Today, there are more than forty thousand ponies registered with the club.

On the open show circuit, many people mistake the versatile POA for its Appaloosa cousin. Since its original breed charter, the pony height requirement has allowed an increase of 4 inches, so in USA Equestrian Pony Hunter classes spectators are frequently surprised and delighted to see this little jumper handily managing the course. Their endurance helps them with the rigorous three-day event, and certain bloodlines have even been seen in the dressage ring.

POAs are often a child's first introduction to the wonderful world of equines. At many summer and ranch camps, kids learn basic horsemanship and riding skills at the hands—or hooves—of these patient, willing ponies. For smaller or younger children, POAs provide confidence and security that taller horses might not give them.

Breed Characteristics

The Pony of the Americas is a larger pony, today standing from 46 to 56 inches at the withers. It must display physical characteristics and an approved coat pattern to be eligible for registration. The POA's head is small and dished, reminiscent of its Arabian forebears. Its body is muscular and powerful looking, like an American Quarter Horse's, and its coloring has to be like that of an Appaloosa. The POA leans more toward "horse" proportions, with ample clean leg under its robust body.

POA coat patterns are as unique as two fingerprints, and often a pony's coat will change with age. One of the most common patterns is the blanket, displaying white over the croup and hips, sometimes dotted by spots. Another is the leopard pattern. POAs of this type are speckled with spots over the entire body. Roan-type Appaloosa markings are also allowed.

The POA was developed specifically as a child's pony, and there are still quite a few restrictions on how adults can be involved competitively with the breed.

Given the POA's talent and versatility, it's hard to keep a good pony "just for the kids". So even though the opportunities for adults are still limited to non-riding disciplines, the club is now looking to relax a few of those rules. And it makes sense, because when kids get involved with POAs they often don't outgrow their love for the pony. They want to stay involved no matter what age they are.

THE RACKING HORSE

THE RACKING HORSE'S GENESIS dates back almost to the birth of America; its history mirrors that of the Tennessee Walking Horse. Renowned for its good looks, resilience, and calm disposition, the horse was used on the plantations in the land of Dixie before the Civil War. It was sought after for its racking gait, which is similar to the Tennessee Walker's running walk, although more collected. The main difference between the two breeds is that the Racking Horse is allowed to perform its gait without special training and without the use of action devices, such as weighted ankle chains. Another difference is that Racking Horses are shown with their tails natural, not artificially set as in some other breeds. Those who spend long hours in the saddle, and need a horse that can be easily sat upon appreciate this effortless horse.

Breed History

In the late 1960s, a group of Alabama businessmen who were involved with the Tennessee Walking Horse set the wheels in motion to have this offshoot of the breed, the Racking Horse, recognized on its own. These were pure Tennessee Walkers, just trained and handled differently, and these men wanted to be able to show their horses in their own breed shows. On May 23, 1971, the USDA recognized the Racking Horse Breeders' Association of America, to perpetuate and protect the Racking Horse breed. A few years later, in 1975, Alabama named it the official state horse.

There are a couple of reasons why Racking Horse enthusiasts felt the need to split from the Tennessee Walking Horse organization. In 1971, a law went into effect called the Horse Protection Act. This act was designed to protect certain

Blessed with beauty and a gentle spirit, the Racking Horse is gaining popularity in and out of the show ring.

breeds of horses from the practice of soring, as well as prosecute those unscrupulous trainers who violated the act. Soring is the unsavory procedure of irritating a horse's feet by various means in order to have him lift his feet high for display in the show ring. Some soring methods merely aggravated the horse, while others caused horrendous pain, and even crippling.

Soring was linked to those who showed the "Big Lick" Tennessee Walkers, horses that wore built-up shoes and chains in order to perform their exaggerated running walk, and this cast a pall over the entire breed. Many people who wanted to disassociate themselves with Walkers opted to turn to the Racking Horse breed to get away from the problems that were plaguing Walkers. But there were financial reasons for the split, too. In order to have a competitive Tennessee Walker under those circumstances, one needed a big bankroll, and many smaller breeders and barns couldn't keep up with the big money flashed in the Walking Horse circles. By starting afresh, the little guy was able to compete quite well with his gaited horse, without having to break the bank.

Breed Characteristics

The Racking Horse is a gracefully built medium-sized horse, standing between 15 and 16 hands high. It has a straight, prominent profile, long, graceful neck, sloping shoulders, long, but well-proportioned back, and slender, flat legs. Its fine-haired coat can be of several color variations, including sorrel, chestnut, black, roan, white, bay, brown, gray, pinto, yellow, dun, palomino, buckskin, champagne, and cremello.

The rack performed is a bilateral four-beat gait that is often called a "single-foot" because only one foot strikes the ground at a time. This rapid, high-stepping gait, comes as standard equipment with the Racking Horse, just as a walk or trot does to other breeds. This rack is not the same as other gaited horses' "racking," which is achieved through training and action devices.

The Racking Horse is both pleasure mount and competitive horse. It can be shown either flat-shod or "padded," with built-up shoes. At the Celebration, held late September every year in Alabama, the cream of the crop is found going head to head in a variety of events. There are classes for trail obstacles, futurities, country pleasure, speed, and the popular Water Glass class, in which the rider

Whether the Racking Horse is flat shod, or shown with pads, he still exhibits the bilateral four beat gait that is smooth and easy to sit.

demonstrates, by not spilling a drop, how smoothly the horse moves. This is a horse for middle-income people to enjoy at home, on trails, and at shows.

It is not a breed found everywhere—yet. Most of the horses are located south of the Mason-Dixon line, and most of those are in Tennessee and Alabama. Beginning riders have found the Racking Horse to be the answer to their prayers, not only for his extremely comfortable ride, but also because of his unusual friendliness to humans. Beginners and veterans alike can be thankful for all that this intelligent, family-oriented Southern belle has to offer.

Famous Racking Horses

Guaranteed Perfect started his career as a World Champion Three Year Old in 1996. The following year, he won the coveted Racking Horse World Grand Championship. He has also shown and competed successfully at the Tennessee Walking Horse Celebration.

Pushoverture was the 2001 grand champion Racking Horse, going from the amateur ranks and regional championships with his owner to the big leagues. Now he stands at stud in Tennessee.

THE ROCKY MOUNTAIN HORSE

WHEN THOUGHTS TURN TO KENTUCKY'S horses, they normally include images of large expanses of white fencing, Thoroughbred broodmares grazing quietly while their foals gambol, and palatial barns in the distance. But that's not the whole picture. While Thoroughbreds are populous in the Bluegrass State, they're not the only cherished equine.

In the early 1900s, a type of gaited horse emerged in the eastern part of the state of Kentucky, near the foothills of the rugged Appalachian Mountains. This Southern treasure is beloved by all who have come to saddle it up and go for a ride. Although small in numbers, its following is fiercely devoted. Today this breed, the Rocky Mountain Horse, is being used for pleasure, on the trail, and for competitive and endurance riding. As a show horse, the breed is rapidly gaining in popularity because of its beauty and unique way of stepping out. Possessing extraordinary natural endurance, Rockys are also surefooted over rough terrain and, because of their gait, they require a minimum of effort by both horse and rider so that together they can cover a great distance without tiring.

The main reason people are so true-blue about their Rocky Mountain horses is not only because of their gentle, wanting-to-please natures, but also for their comfortable, ambling, four-beat gait. Because the horse was such a smooth mover, folks in the Appalachian Mountains selected it to work the farms nestled in the rugged foothills. But this was not merely a workhorse. Even though the Rocky Mountain Horse could easily handle all the plowing and cattle work of the farms, he also doubled as the snappy transportation needed to get into town on the weekend. The horse's temperament was even ideal for the farmer's kids to

Hailing from the Appalachians of Kentucky, the Rocky Mountain Horse is known as a robust, all-around horse.

ride. Its gentle attitude became legendary. And talk about an easy keeper. Unlike some of its delicate cousins, the Rocky Mountain horse didn't require warm, air-tight stables to flourish through the winter. Even during the frigid, snowy winters in the foothills, this horse could tolerate the cold just fine.

Breed History

A young stallion, whose name is not recorded, bearing a chocolate-colored coat and flaxen mane and tail, was born in the early 1900s in Kentucky's Appalachians. He was brought to the eastern portion of the state where his owners began using him as a breeding stallion to cover their Kentucky-bred mares. His foals also bore his unique coloring, and had his wonderful nature and unique four-beat gait, to boot. With subsequent breedings it became clear that these horses of the Kentucky Mountains, isolated by their geography, were an actual type.

A few years later, a breeder named Sam Tuttle bought a Rocky Mountain mare and used her to produce several foals, which he used on his trail string at the Kentucky Natural Bridge State Park. One colt, christened Old Tobe, was a fine specimen of the Mountain Horse, and became the foundation stallion of the breed. And the Rocky Mountain rental horses? They began to garner interest from the public, who were quite taken with this medium-sized horse with the effortless gaits and the silky dark coat.

Over the years, more people began referring to this horse as a breed, with its own genotype. And people began crossing their other horses to the Rocky Mountains. Many breeds, when they have their gene pool diluted with the blood of other horses, suffer. However, the Rocky Mountain horse was able to retain its main characteristics and its conformation. But, with no breed registry, no record-keeping, and haphazard breeding practices, the breed was in danger of losing what purity it had. If the horses did not have a studbook—an official registry to maintain and promote the breed—the horse might disappear from the face of the earth. So in 1986, a group of enthusiasts formed the Rocky Mountain Horse Association (RMHA). They

Possessing a natural single-foot gait, the Rocky Mountain Horse is not trained with any special equipment to enhance its gait.

worked to locate individual Rocky Mountain Horses scattered throughout Kentucky, Indiana, and Ohio. The organization sought to find ways to increase the horses' small numbers, as well as let the rest of the world in on this well-kept secret from the South. Lastly, the organization established the breed's official characteristics.

Breed Characteristics

Rockys usually stand between 14.2 and 16 hands tall, with most ranging right around 15 hands. They have a wide chest, a graceful, sloping shoulder, and compact frame. They possess a straight profile, with kind, expressive eyes, and well-proportioned ears. Rockys also bear a graceful, arched neck, proportionate to the body and set at an angle for naturally upright carriage. Many say that it is apparent that Rockys have Spanish forebears, since their appearance is often similar to Iberian horses. They sport a solid body color, although a little white on the face is okay as long as it isn't overwhelming. Legs can also be white up to the knee or hock. Most are a rich, dark chestnut—almost a chocolate color—with a flaxen mane and tail. The horse also is required to have its trademark even temper and willing nature.

Rockys are particularly popular with older adults who look at their equine partners as trusted companions in leisure pursuits. Rockys are great for novices who are just finding their feet in the horse world, but competitive riders are also drawn to their versatility and ability to perform.

As important as its beautiful looks and conformation is its way of going. A Rocky has to have a natural ambling four-beat gait, with no lateral pacing. This means that when the horse goes into its gait, you can count four distinct hoof beats that are similar to the cadence of the walk. Their gaits allow them to travel at a good clip, going anywhere from seven to even twenty miles an hour when they're really flying. Their gait shouldn't be enhanced by training aids or built-up shoeing, and the

Rockys are known for being gentle and affectionate toward people.

COMPARABLE BREED

The Icelandic Horse has served the people of this remote island for more than a thousand years, carrying them over rough countryside and across lava fields and fast-flowing rivers. The breed displays five unique gaits, including the tolt, a four-beat running walk, and the pace, a speedy smooth trot in which the legs move in lateral, not diagonal, pairs.

breed association doesn't allow soring of the horse to produce artificial front-end action, either.

During the late 1980s, a genetics researcher looked at one hundred foundation horses in order to establish the breed's genetic identity. He found five unique markers indicating pure bloodlines that were a result of the breed's isolation in the Appalachian foothills. Because of this seclusion, the horse maintained its own unique appearance, and an unusual way of going.

Today, more and more folks are drawn to the Rocky Mountain Horse because of its model-horse coloring, its personality, and easy, floating single-foot gait. There has been increased awareness of the breed, and with that an increase in demand as well, with many breeders needing to put clients on waiting lists for their spring crop of babies.

Rockies are surefooted and sensible on the trail, and because of this, more are participating each year in events such as competitive trail riding and even endurance. But make no mistake—they can also perform in the show ring under the lights in a variety of disciplines.

The International Rocky Mountain Horse Show is held in September at the Kentucky Horse Park, with Lexington's rolling green fields as an elegant backdrop.

Rocky Mountain Horses have a plethora of classes to help display the breed's versatility. Competing in rail classes, such as western and English pleasure, as well as games events like pole bending, they also have classes in which to show off the breed's trademark gait. The Rocky Mountain Horse is judged at the show walk, the Rocky Mountain pleasure gait, and the trail walk.

The show walk is described as a deliberate four-beat lateral gait performed at medium speed with a smooth, even rhythm. The horse moves with activity, but not speed. In dressage circles, you might describe it as the horse's "working walk." When the horse shifts into his pleasure gait, he shows greater action and speed than at the show walk. The trail walk is different still—it is calm, relaxed, and natural. It is performed on a loose rein and natural headset, and the horse will be penalized if he shows nervousness or agitation.

Rocky Mountain Horses cannot be shown with exaggerated weighted shoes or artificial training or action devices, and are considered a natural breed. Rocky enthusiasts wish to preserve it as close to the real McCoy as possible, keeping it part of the South's legacy. Rich gaits, rich color, rich history. The Rocky Mountain Horse provides its riders with Southern comfort unlike any other.

Famous Rocky Mountain Horses

Old Tobe, who was owned by Rocky Mountain Horse breeder Sam Tuttle in the early 1900s, was a rent-string horse at the Kentucky Natural Bridge State Park for most of his life, taking novice riders over the rough Kentucky terrain. But he was also a stallion, and produced foals that were nearly identical to him. Considered the official foundation stallion of the breed, he lived to be thirty-seven years old. His name can be found in the pedigree of every Rocky Mountain Horse.

THE STANDARDBRED

WE ALL KNOW THAT THE THOROUGHBRED is the fastest distance horse on four legs, but if you had to hold him to a trot, could he surpass all others? The answer to that is most certainly no—that title goes to the quickest trotting horse in the world, the Standardbred. With lightning speed performed at a two-beat gait, this horse, known mostly as a harness racer, has also been used to improve other breeds of racing trotters and pacers around the globe. But that's not where the horse's only talents lie. Today, more and more horses are finding their way into the hearts of regular riders, and finding new careers away from the racetrack.

The name Standardbred was first used in 1879, and it refers to the fact that harness racers had to prove they could trot a mile within the standard time of 2 minutes, 30 seconds in order to be registered. Modern Standardbreds, with their improved bloodlines and training, have since smashed that old requirement to bits, often racing a mile in as little as 1 minute, 50 seconds.

Breed History

The earliest harness racers in the Americas were the Narragansett Pacer and the Canadian Pacer, which raced in New England in the eighteenth century. English Thoroughbreds were crossed with these and several other breeds, including the Norfolk Trotter, the Hackney, the Morgan, and the Canadian Pacer, creating a horse that became known for its two distinctive racing gaits.

The original trotting races in the eighteenth century were simply held in fields, and the horses were actually raced under saddle. However, farmers and breeders began to take their match races pretty seriously, and by the mid–1700s, trotting racers were held on official courses, this time with the horses in harness.

Nearly all Standardbreds are bred for the harness-racing track, not as pleasure mounts.

Trotting is a natural gait for horses, but the Standardbred does so with amazing speed.

Breeders quickly moved to improve their trotters, and selected bloodlines that could produce even more speed from their horses. In 1788, Messenger, a gray Thoroughbred stallion, was brought to America from England. The Thoroughbreds during this era actually had bloodlines similar to the Norfolk Roadster, and Messenger was a prime example of this breeding. He became one of the most influential sires of racers; producing both runners and trotters, with the trotters possessing great action, speed, and heart.

In 1849, Hambletonian, a descendant of Messenger, was born out of a crippled bay mare that had been bred to the ungainly, belligerent stallion Abdullah. Sold as a cast-off, Hambletonian astounded everyone, and proved to be a prolific sire. His offspring, too, were natural trotting athletes. Today nearly every trotter and pacer can trace its lineage back to this remarkable stud of humble origins.

Breed Characteristics

The Standardbred is both like and unlike its cousin, the Thoroughbred. Although typically a little shorter, standing anywhere from 14.2 to 16 hands high, and slightly stockier than the long, leggy "Blood Horse," Standardbreds have similar refined legs, powerful shoulders and hindquarters, and a medium to longish back. It has a unique, straight, or sometimes squarish profile to its face—a little less refined than most Thoroughbreds. Standardbreds are built sound and sturdy, and unlike some Thoroughbreds, which have large feet, their hooves are in nice proportion to their bodies. Most are usually bay or brown, but other coat colors can be found, including chestnut, strawberry roan, and gray.

Racing Standardbreds have two gaits: the trot and the pace. The pace is a lateral gait, in which both legs on one side of the body move together. In the trot, the legs move in diagonal pairs. Pacers are born with the inclination to pace, yet also trot when they're not racing, so pacers are trained and raced with "hopples," straps linking the front and back legs on each side to keep them moving in unison.

Standardbreds begin their racing careers at two years of age, with pacers competing against pacers and trotters competing in trotting races. Many breeders and trainers believe that trotters take a little more time to come up to speed and develop fully, which is why there are more racing pacers than trotters—by a margin of four to one. Whether trotting or pacing, Standardbreds can reach speeds of up to thirty-five miles an hour and tend to reserve their greatest burst of speed for the final quarter of the race. If a horse breaks his gait while racing, whether he is a trotter or a pacer, the driver must bring the horse back and "lose ground" to the other racers before he can continue the race. But Standardbreds are not only raced in harness. There is a small contingent of fans who still enjoy under-saddle trotting and pacing races, a reflection of the breed's past.

Many think of the Standardbred only as a harness racer, but the breed takes part in a host of other riding and driving events. The Standardbred Pleasure Horse Organization, founded in America in the 1980s, helps to support the breed in other riding and driving disciplines. With nine chapters throughout the nation helping promote ex-racers for more traditional equestrian pursuits such as dressage and jumping, they are dispelling common Standardbred stereotypes. And they are also very keen to help new owners enjoy their horses to the fullest, including sponsoring "retraining clinics" on a regular basis.

The breed has the usual natural gaits all horses have, and pacers can even be retrained to trot. Cantering and jumping comes just as naturally to Standardbreds as any other breed, and they can be seen tackling cross-country courses, making the rounds in show jumping, and executing flawless dressage tests (often mistaken, yes, for Thoroughbreds). You'll find them in open shows, but there are also Standardbred breed shows where the ex-racers compete against their own kind in a host of western and English classes. The races for Standardbreds don't have the money or the prestige of Thoroughbred racing, but two events, the Little Brown Jug and the Hambeltonian, are coveted races that Standardbreds aspire to.

Because harness racers travel around the country during the racing season, they can handle a busy schedule and commotion without getting ruffled. Unlike the Thoroughbred, they possess a more even temperament which makes them good ranch horses and excellent trail mounts. Surefooted and level-headed, these former racehorses are often sought after by endurance riders as an option, but it's their stamina that clinches the deal for these intense competitors.

There are also a good many Standardbreds in Amish country, for two simple reasons: they are already comfortable between the shafts of a buggy, and they are plentiful and inexpensive at local auctions.

In pacing, the Standardbred's legs move in lateral pairs, which gives the gait a rolling motion. Some bloodlines are naturally inclined to pace.

While one might think moving to the country would be an idyllic life for a former racer, it's actually one that has some challenges, as the Amish ride along busy country highways on hard pavement day after day. Horses are a utilitarian means to an end, so they don't always get the love and care owners should provide. Still, it's the Standardbred's willing, affable personality that makes him want to please whatever owner he has.

Famous Standardbreds

Dan Patch was one of the most famous pacers in history. He broke world records at least fourteen times in the early 1900s. Dan Patch only lost two heats in his career and never lost a race. Dan Patch's official record of 1:55¼ for the pacing mile was set in 1905 at the Red Mile track in Lexington, Kentucky.

The Standardbred is somewhat stockier and more muscular than its racing cousin, the Thoroughbred.

COMPARABLE BREED

The French Trotter is also a major player when it comes to harness racing. It is more robust than its American counterpart and is sometimes used for other events such as jumping and general riding. Although there is no standard conformation, they range in type from those closely resembling the Thoroughbred in appearance, to a stronger, sturdier horse with straighter shoulders and more rounded action.

Rambling Willie, a bay pacer gelding, earned over $2 million during his career and retired at age thirteen. He was voted Champion Aged Pacer of the Year three times in a row from 1975 to 1977. He had the most starts and the most wins by any Standardbred, and retired as the richest Standardbred in history.

Although Standardbreds are only produced for the track, they are in need of individuals willing to give them a chance at a new life once their career is over. One has to only meet a Standardbred to see this is a horse of fortitude; a tough little character with so much heart. Those who have introduced these former racers to careers out of the traces find that they themselves learn valuable lessons about starting anew and the importance of second chances.

THE TENNESSEE WALKING HORSE

THE TECHNIQUE OF POSTING THE TROT was developed in England, probably around the 1700s. Legend has it that letter carriers had to come up with a way to make the trot, a rather bouncy, two-beat gait, a tolerable one after many hours in the saddle, day in and day out. Had they ridden Tennessee Walking Horses, however, they would have never needed to create such a method. Because of the Tennessee Walker's amazingly effortless gaits that have earned them the nickname, "the Glide Ride," the breed has introduced both first timers and seasoned veterans to a delightful world of easy riding.

Breed History

In the late 1800s, in central Tennessee, the kernels of a breed were being sown. Settlers from states such as Virginia, North Carolina, and South Carolina decided to make a new home in Tennessee. Some brought their Morgans, while others brought Canadian Horses, Narragansett Pacers, or perhaps Thoroughbreds. Soon the settlers were buying each other's horses or their stud's services, and began to combine these bloodlines. The resulting horses took many fine characteristics from this large gene pool, resulting in saddle horses that were robust, yet elegant, with upright conformation and unusual gaiting ability.

These crossbreds were created as a multipurpose workhorse. They performed light work on the farms and plantations, but they also drove the family wagon, took the farmer to town under saddle, and gave the kids a ride on weekends. Their easy-to-sit gaits were a requirement, since farmers spent hours in the saddle riding fence lines and checking fields. Soon, professionals such as doctors,

The profile of the Tennessee Walking Horse is one that is often described as noble, with a straight or sometimes slightly convex contour.

attorneys, and clergymen were seeking out the abilities of these dark, attractive horses with the ground-covering, gliding gait.

It was this trademark, the running walk, which became the Tennessee Walker's claim to fame. The running walk is something the Walker is born with. This high-stepping four-beat gait eats up the ground like a canter, but each foot falls independently, as in the walk. A rider on a Walker simply feels as though the horse is sliding across the ground effortlessly. The horse's head bobs gently, and he will overstep, meaning that his back hoof prints will make marks ahead of where the front ones hit. And the running walk is just that: a speedy gait that can reach up to twenty miles an hour—which a Walker can perform for miles without tiring.

Over the next few decades, breeders sought to bring this gait out even further by sticking to stallions that consistently produced horses with the running walk. A registry, The Tennessee Walking Horse Breeder's Association of America was formed in 1935, and a stallion, Black Allan, was selected as the foundation horse for the breed. Black Allan, who was born many years before in 1885, was part Morgan and part Standardbred, and could trace back some of his bloodlines to the legendary foundation Standardbred Hambletonian. Black Allen contributed style and stamina to many generations of horses, and even today his legacy continues, with his bloodlines found in a majority of modern Walkers.

It's not just the potpourri of bloodlines that combine to make the Walker so special. Even their environment factored into their hardiness, their durability. The Middle Basin of Tennessee is rich in minerals, from the water sources to the grasslands, which has resulted in hard bone, solid feet, and a long, healthy life span.

Breed Characteristics

Tennessee Walkers have such a distinct look—almost an air about them—that even if you didn't see them in action, you would still easily identify them. Usually dark bay or even black (although they are seen in a variety of

The running walk is seen in some show horses, and is enhanced with weighted pastern chains and pads on the hooves.

colors including chestnut, roan, palomino, gray and even spotted) the horses stand fairly tall—between 15 and 16 hands high, and weigh 900 to 1,200 pounds. Sporting a large, intelligent head with a straight profile, swiveling ears, ample nostrils, and bright eyes, it has a well-proportioned, slightly arched neck that comes up from a sloping shoulder. The horse has a short back, powerful haunches, and long, clean legs with strong hooves.

Besides the running walk, the horse also performs two other gaits. He has a four-beat "flat-foot walk" which is more of a marching, medium walk, as well as a canter, similar to a gallop in hand with a rolling, rocking horse motion. And while the running walk is what the horse is renowned for, the other gaits are just as easy and pleasurable to sit. Some are even able to perform the rack, stepping pace, fox trot, single foot, and other variations of the famous running walk. These aren't asked for in the show ring, but are smooth, easy gaits that work well on the trail.

Flat-shod Tennessee Walking Horses are often called Plantation Walkers, and are not exhibited with action devices.

COMPARABLE BREED

Truthfully, one would be hard-pressed to find a horse outside of the United States that is comparable to the Tennessee Walker. The Orlov Trotter, a Russian trotting breed, is a horse that has beauty, tractability, and endurance. Standing about 15 hands tall, Orlovs are often seen pulling troikas, a Russian type of sled.

Many breeds boast that their horses are tractable and willing, but the Walking Horse truly does want to please and doesn't have a mean bone in its body. More folks are finding that the Walker is a perfect partner for pleasure, trail, and recreation, which is different from the picture that most people envision when they first think of the breed. So while a high-stepping horse performing the exaggerated gaits in the show ring is one aspect of the breed, it's not the only one.

For those with competition in mind, the Tennessee Walker's breed show is indeed a Celebration. Each year, on the Saturday night before Labor Day, the best Walking Horses vie for the Grand Champion title. Since 1939, the breed association, known since 1974 as the Tennessee Walking Horse Breeder's and Exhibitor's Association (TWHBEA) has been holding their Tennessee Walking Horse National Celebration in Shelbyville, Tennessee, to honor the best of the best in the Walking world.

The Tennessee Walking Horse is shown both under saddleseat and in western tack and attire. There are divisions for both built-up, or padded, and flat-shod horses.

The flat-shod segment has grown by leaps and bounds, since the horses are delightfully easy to train, and because their gaits come so naturally. This is a division for the individual who doesn't want to go out and hire a big-name trainer in order to be competitive.

The flat-shod plantation pleasure horse should display brilliance and show presence in the ring, as well as be well-mannered and easily managed. He is judged at his walking horse gaits, and if he paces, racks, or breaks into a trot, he'll be counted down. A nod in the head, sometimes penalized in other riding disciplines, is actually important. They say, "if he isn't nodding, he isn't walking."

Western pleasure entries want to display their Walking Horse as a western working horse, exhibiting an exceptionally smooth, comfortable ride without excessive animation. A good western pleasure horse should have a balanced, flowing motion with a free and easy gait.

The performance Tennessee Walking Horse, sometimes referred to as padded or built-up, is shown only in English saddleseat attire and tack. It executes the basic gaits with much more animation and accentuated brilliance.

Performance horses of the Walking Horse breed are commonly shown with double-nailed and triple-nailed pads to add dimension of the hoof, which accentuates and exaggerates the way the horse gaits. Pads are an integral part of the training of the performance Tennessee Walking Horse, and their effectiveness and usefulness will vary with each individual horse.

The performance division is the one that the horse is most often depicted in and, unfortunately, it is the one that has cost the Tennessee Walker its reputation for many years due to unscrupulous behavior by some trainers and owners.

Because showing the performance Walkers, known as "big lick" horses, attracted big money, several decades ago trainers who wanted an "edge" to win thought that the way to get their horses to raise their feet higher was to irritate them. A horse that was annoyed by what he felt under his feet, or around his ankles, would undoubtedly snap his legs up to avoid that sensation. Trainers went beyond the normal, permitted action devices such as the padded shoes and the weighted chains. The process was known as "soring the horse," making him sore enough to, well, soar. It was not unusual for horses to be crippled by some of the most extreme methods, all in the name of man's vanity.

In 1971 the government enacted the Horse Protection Act to prohibit any person from soring any breed of horse. Designated Qualified Persons would check for compliance at shows, which was very difficult to enforce. As the years went by the public became more aware of the soring issue. Breed members splintered off from the breed organization, beginning their own divisions for

Tennessee Walkers have a large presence, but are medium-sized horses with good bone and sturdy conformation.

flat-shod, or "plantation" walkers. In the 1990s, the TWHBEA rallied to the cause to put in better regulations and enforcement. They also became more proactive with their members, promoting soundness in horses. The organization continues to work diligently to get its name back in good standing with the equine industry, with animal welfare advocates, and with the general public. Today the TWHBEA has made great strides in reducing the amount of violations that are committed, as well as promoting their horse for what it truly is: a remarkable, people-loving animal that enriches its handler's lives.

So what is the future of this creature? As more newbies are introduced to horses, it seems that Tennessee Walkers are an ideal breed. Forgiving, versatile, willing, and comfortable—these characteristics are why the young and old, the novice and veteran, find they are in a Tennessee state of mind.

Famous Tennessee Walkers

Allen's Gold Zephyr, a palomino Tennessee Walker, was also known as Trigger Junior, and belonged to Roy Rogers. The horse was taught a variety of tricks, including rearing and bowing. The horse that played Silver in *The Lone Ranger* television series of the 1950s was reportedly a Tennessee Walking Horse as well.

The First Grand Champion Walking Horse of the World was crowned in 1939. **Strolling Jim** helped put Walkers on the map; the most rapid growth of the breed took place during the years when Jim was in his prime.

Sundust was put into training as a two-year-old, but due to an injury was put out to stud in the late 1950s. He sired many champion show horses and his broodmares were prized.

Merry Walker was a supreme broodmare, producing fabulous Walking Horses in the mid 1950s. She was the only mare to foal two world grand champions: **Go Boys Shadow** and **Rodgers Perfection.**

BREED ASSOCIATIONS

American White and American Creme
   Horse Registry
Route 1, Box 20
Naper, NE 68755-2020
(402) 832-5560

American Azteca Horse International
   Association
2218 Jackson Blvd. #3 PMB 901
Rapid City, SD 57702-3452
(605) 342-2322
www.americanazteca.com

Appaloosa Horse Club
2720 W. Pullman Road
Moscow, ID 83843
(208) 882-5578
www.appaloosa.com

Appaloosa Sport Horse Association
3380 Saxonburg Blvd.
Glenshaw, PA 15116
(412) 767-4616

International Colored Appaloosa
   Association
P.O. Box 99
Shipshewana, IN 46565
(574) 825-3331
www.icaainc.com

International Curly Horse Organization
2690 Carpenter Road
Jamestown, OH 45335
(937) 453-9829
www.curlyhorses.org

American Bashkir Curly Registry
P.O. Box 246
Ely, NV 89301-0246
(775) 289-4999
www.abcregistry.org

American Buckskin Registry Association
P.O. Box 3850
Redding, CA 96049-3850
(530) 223-1420
www.americanbuckskin.org

International Buckskin Horse
   Association
P.O. Box 268
Shelby, IN 46377-0268
(219) 552-1013
www.ibha.net

International Champagne Horse
   Registry
P.O. Box 4430
Paso Robles, CA 93447
www.champagne-horse-assoc.org

Colorado Ranger Horse
  Association
RD 1, Box 1290
Wampum, PA 16157-9610
(724) 535-4841
www.coloradoranger.com

Florida Cracker Horse Association
P.O. Box 186
Newberry, FL 32669-0186
(352) 472-2228

American Cream Draft Horse
  Association
2065 Noble Ave.
Charles City, IA 50616-9108
(641) 228-5308
www.americancreamdraft.org

American Cream Draft Horse
  Foundation
38175 Montezuma Valley Road
Box B-3
Ranchita, CA 92006
(760) 782-3704

Harnessbred Breeders Affiliation
8481 Elm Creek Road
Moody, TX 76557
(254) 853-3744

American Indian Horse Registry
 9028 State Park Road
Lockhart, TX 78644-9713
(512) 398-6642

American Miniature Horse
  Association Inc.
5601 S. I-35 W.
Alvarado, TX 76009
(817) 783-5600
www.amha.com

American Miniature Horse Registry
81-B E. Queenwood
Morton, IL 61550
(309) 263-4044

International Miniature Trotting and
  Pacing Association
18481 Elm Creek Road
Moody, TX 76557
(254) 853-3744

Missouri Fox Trotting Horse Breed
  Association Inc.
P.O. Box 1027
Ava, MO 65608-1027
(417) 683-2468
www.mfthba.com

International Morab Breeders
  Association and Registry
RR 3, Box 235
Ava, MO 65608
(417) 683-4426
www.morab.com

Purebred Morab Horse Association/
  Purebred Morab Horse Registry
P.O. Box 10
Sherwood, WI 54169
(920) 853-3086
www.morabnet.com

American Morgan Horse Association
P.O. Box 960
Shelburne, VT 05482-0960
(802) 985-4944
www.morganhorse.com

Lippitt Morgan Breeders' Association
360 S3361, Hwy. 67
Dousman, WI 53118
(530) 633-9271

Mountain Pleasure Horse
   Association
P.O. Box 79
Wellington, KY 40387
(859) 768-9224

North American Mustang
   Association and Registry
P.O. Box 850906
Mesquite, TX 75185-0906
(972) 289-9344

American Mustang and Burro
   Association
P.O. Box 788
Lincoln, CA 95648
(530) 633-9271

Midwest Kiger Mustang
   Registry
1472 N. Shaytown Road
Vermontville, MI 49096-9541
(517) 726-1226

National Native American Gaited
   Horse Registry
P.O. Box 4326
N. Fort Meyers, FL 33917
(941) 543-5252

American Paint Horse
   Association
P.O. Box 961023
Fort Worth, TX 76161-0023
(817) 834-2742
www.apha.com

Palomino Horse Association
HC 63, Box 24
Dornsife, PA 17823
(570) 758-3067
www.palominohorseassoc.com

Palomino Horse Breeders of
   America
15253 E. Skelly Drive
Tulsa, OK 74116-2637
(918) 438-1234
www.palominohba.com

American Part-Blooded Horse
   Registry
4120 S.E. River Drive
Portland, OR 97267-6899
(503) 654-6204

Pony of the Americas Club
5240 Elmwood Ave.
Indianapolis, IN 46203-5990
(317) 788-0107
www.poac.org

American Quarter Horse Association
P.O. Box 200
Amarillo, TX 79168-0001
(806) 376-4811
www.aqha.com

Foundation Quarter Horse Registry
Box 230
Sterling, CO 80751
(970) 522-7822

National Foundation Quarter Horse
   Association
P.O. Box P
Joseph, OR 97846
(541) 426-4403
www.nfqha.com

Racking Horse Breeders Association
   of America
67 Horse Center Road
Decatur, AL 35603
(256) 353-7225

Rocky Mountain Horse
    Association
P.O. Box 129
Mt. Olivet, KY 41064
(606) 724-2354
www.rmhorse.com

American Saddlebred Horse
    Association
4093 Iron Works Pkwy.
Lexington, KY 40511-8434
(859) 259-2742
www.saddlebred.com

Half-Saddlebred Registry of
    America
4093 Iron Works Pkwy.
Lexington, KY 40511-8434
(859) 259-2742

National Show Horse Registry
10368 Bluegrass Pkwy.
Louisville, KY 40299
(502) 266-5100
www.nshregistry.org

American Show Pony Registry
81-B E. Queenwood Road
Morton, IL 61550
(309) 263-4044

Spanish Mustang Registry
11790 Halstad Ave. S
Lonsdale, MN 55046
(507) 744-2704
www.spanishmustang.org

Federation of North American
    Sport Horse Registries
939 Merchandise Mart
Chicago, IL 60654
(312) 527-6544

International Sport Horses of
    Color
P.O. Box 294
Newcastle, CA 95658
(916) 645-6909
www.shoc.org

Sport Horse Owners and
    Breeders Association
PMB 241
6753 Thomasville Road,
    Suite 108
Tallahassee, FL 32312-3837
(850) 893-8532
www.sport-horse.org

Standardbred Pleasure Horse
    Organization
87 Round Hill Road
Northampton, MA 01060
(302) 349-9296
www.spho.net

United States Trotting
    Association
750 Michigan Ave.
Columbus, OH 43215-1191
(614) 224-2291
www.ustrotting.com

Tennessee Walking Horse Breeders'
    and Exhibitors' Association
P.O. Box 286
Lewisburg, TN 37091-0286
(931) 359-1574

Walking Horse Owners'
    Association of America
1535 W. Northfield Blvd.
Murfreesboro, TN 37129
 (615) 890-9120
www.walkinghorseowners.com

Part Walking Horse Registry
HC 84, Box 3087
Forsythe, MT 59327
(406) 356-2854
www.hiplainswalkers.com

International Trotting and
Pacing Association
513 Broadmore Estates
Goshen, IN 46528-6331
(219) 534-6989

Walkaloosa Horse Association
2995 Clark Valley Road
Los Osos, CA 93402
(805) 528-7308
www.walkaloosaregistry.com

American Walking Pony
Registry
P.O. Box 5282
Macon, GA 31208-5282
(912) 743-2321

American Warmblood Registry
P.O. Box 1236
Jackson, CA 95642
(209) 245-3565
www.americanwarmblood.com

American Warmblood Society
2 Buffalo Run Road
Center Ridge, AR 72027-8347
(501) 893-2777
www.americanwarmblood.org

INDEX

A

Adios Amigos, 17

Adopt-A-Horse program. *See* Mustang

Albinism, in horses. *See* American White

Allen's Gold Zephyr, 199

American Albino Horse Club, 47–48

American Bashkir Curly Register, 75, 201

American Celebrated Running Quarter Horse, 22

American Cream Draft Horse, 2, 3–8
breed characteristics, 4, 6–7
breed history, 3–6
comparable breed, 5

American Cream Draft Horse Association, 4, 202

American Creme. *See also* American White
breed characteristics, 48–50, 49

American Horse, 32

American Miniature Horse Association, 103, 202

American Minor Breeds Conservancy, 5

American Morgan Horse Association, 128, 202

American Morgan Horse Register, 128

American Paint Horse, 8, 9–17
adaptability of, 14, 15–17
breed characteristics, 11, 12, 12–13, 15, 16
breed history, 9–12
comparable breed, 13
famous horses, 17

American Paint Horse Association (APHA), 11–12, 15–16, 203

American Palomino Horse Registry, 159

American Quarter Horse, 18, 19–29
and American Paint, 10–11
and Appaloosa, 58
and Azteca, 65, 67–68
breed characteristics, 21, 24, 24–28, 27, 28
breed history, 20–23, 23
celebrity fans of, 28–29
comparable breed, 26
and Cracker Horse, 97
famous horses, 29
and Morgan, 129
and Palomino, 160

American Quarter Horse Association (AQHA), 10–11, 22–23, 25, 26–28, 203

American Royal, 38

American Saddlebred, 30, 31–43
breed characteristics, 34, 35, 37–38
breed history, 31–32, 34–35
comparable breed, 40
enthusiasts of, 43
famous horses, 40, 41, 42–43
and Missouri Fox Trotter, 110
and Morgan, 129
and National Show Horse, 147–48, 151–52
and Palomino, 159
sports and specialties of, 33, 36, 37, 38–42, 39, 42

American Saddlebred Horse Association
(ASHA), 35, 151, 154, 203–4
American White, 44, 45–51
breed characteristics, 46, 48–50,
49
breed history, 45, 47–48
famous horses, 50–51
Amish, and Standardbred, 187–88
Andalusian, 53, 95
and Azteca, 65, 67, 68
Apache Double, 63
Appaloosa, 52, 53–63
adaptability of, 58, 59, 60–61, 62
breed characteristics, 54, 56, 58
breed history, 53, 55–58
comparable breed, 61
famous horses, 61, 63
and Pony of the Americas, 166–67,
168
Appaloosa Horse Club (ApHC), 57,
61, 201
Appaloosa Sport Horse Association,
60, 201
Appendix horses, 25
Arabian
and Colorado Ranger Horse,
89–90
and Morab, 117, 119
and National Show Horse, 147–48,
151–52, 153
Arabian Horse Registry of America,
151, 154
Assateague Island. *See* Chincoteague
Pony
Associations, breed, 201–5
Australian Stock Horse, 26
Azteca, 64, 65–70
breed description, 68–70, 69
breed history, 65, 66, 67–68
comparable breed, 68
famous horses, 70
Azteca Horse Owner Association, 65
Azteca Horse Registry of America, 65

B
Bamboo Harvester, 43
Barb, 95
Bashkir Curly, 71, 72, 73–77
breed description, 74, 75–76
breed history, 73–75
comparable breed, 76
famous horses, 76–77
Becerra, Ramon, 70
Beechnut, 28–29
Belgian, 5
Black Allan, 192
Black Beauty, 29
Black Hand, 166
The Black Stallion, 29
BLM. *See* Bureau of Land Management
(BLM)
Boomhower, Les, 165–66
Brabant, 5
Breed associations, 201–5
Bright Zip, 61
Brimmers, 109
Brinkley, Christie, 28
Brumby, 142
Buck No. 4, 3
Bureau of Land Management (BLM),
136, 137, 138, 141
Buttercup, 159

C
Canadian Pacer, and Standardbred, 183
Cattle, breeds for working
American Paint Horse, 14, 15
American Quarter Horse, 22, 67
Azteca, 67–68
Colorado Ranger Horse, 90
Florida Cracker Horse, 96
Morab, 121
Chester Dare, 115
Chickasaw Pony, 10, 20
Chincoteague Pony, 78, 79–87
breed characteristics, 85–87, 86

breed history, 79–81, 82, 83, 84–85
comparable breed, 84
famous ponies, 81, 87
Chincoteague Volunteer Fire
    Department, 80–84
Cincinnati, 43
Cisco Kid SF, 154
Civil War, breeds ridden in
    American Saddlebred, 34, 43
    Morgans, 125
Classic Curly Riders, 76
Cloud, 145
Cloud, Wild Stallion of the Rockies,
    145
Colorado Ranger Horse, 88, 89–93
    breed characteristics, 90, 91, 92,
        92–93
    breed history, 89–90
Comanche, 132
Conquistadors, arrival of, x
    and Azteca, 65, 67
    and Palomino, 159
    and pintos, 9–10
Cortes, Hernando, 9
Costner, Kevin, 29
Cothran, E. Gus, 5
Cracker Horses, 20, 96–97
Crop-outs, 25
Crystal, Billy, 28–29
Cuddles, 107
Cyclone, 87

D

Damele, Peter, 73
Dances with Wolves, 29
Dan Patch, 188
Dash For Cash, 29
Dawn Horse, ix–x
DC Magic, 154
Doc's Keepin' Time, 29
Drafts. *See* American Cream
    Draft Horse

Dressage, breeds in
    American Saddlebred, 42
    Appaloosa, 60
    Azteca, 67–68
    Bashkir Curly, 75, 76–77
    Morab, 121
    Morgan, 131, 132
    National Show Horse, 152
    Palomino, 163
    Standardbred, 187

E

English Thoroughbred
    and American Quarter Horse,
        20–22, 25
    and American Saddlebred, 32
    and Appaloosa, 58
    and Miniature Horse, 103
    and Morgan, 123
    and Standardbred, 183, 185
Eohippus, ix–x
Equus, x
Ethan Allen, 125
Evans, Dale, 159
Evolution, of horse, ix–x
    spotted horses, 53
Explorers, Spanish. *See* Conquistadors,
    arrival of

F

Falabella, 101, 103
Fanny Jenks, 125
Ferdowsi, 58
Fields, Samuel, 80
Figure, 123–25
Florida Cracker Horse, 94, 95–99
    breed characteristics, 96, 98–99
    breed history, 95–98
    comparable breed, 98
Florida Cracker Horse Association,
    97, 201

French Anglo-Arab, 119
French Trotter, 189
Friesian, 129
Fuller, Martha Doyle, 118

G
Gaits, of breeds
    American Saddlebred, 34–35, 38–40,
       39
    Icelandic Horse, 180
    Missouri Fox Trotter, 109–10, 110,
       114, 114
    Morgan, 131–32
    National Show Horse, 151
    Racking Horse, 172
    Rocky Mountain Horse, 175, 177,
       178, 181
    Standardbred, 185, 187
    Tennessee Walking Horse, 191–92,
       193, 194
Go Boys Shadow, 199
Godolphin Barb, 20
Golddust, 117–18
Golden Governor, 115
Grant, Ulysses S., 43, 89
Great Belles of Fire, 43
Guaranteed Perfect, 173
Guide horses, 104, 107

H
Hacas, 65, 67
Hackney, 40, 152
Haines, Frances, 57
Hambletonian, 185
Hamid, Sultan, 89
Harness racing, and Standardbred, 182,
   183–87, 184, 186
Hearst, William Randolph, 118
Henry, Marguerite, 79, 87
Heza Night Train, 17
Highland Dale, 43

Hightower, 29
Horse Protection Act, 171–72, 196
The Horse Whisperer, 29
The Horse with the Flying Tail, 159
Huntington, Rudolf, 89
Hyperkalemic periodic paralysis, 26

I
Imperator, 40, 41
Impressive, 26
Indian Pony. *See* Appaloosa
International Albino Association, 45
International American Albino
    Association (IAAA), 48
International Morab Breeder's
    Association, 119, 202
International Society for the Protection
    of Mustangs & Burros, 137
I Prefer Montana, 43

J
Jackson, Stonewall, 43
Janus, 20–22
JB Andrew, 145
Jennet, 95
Jewel, 28
Johnson, Velma, 137
Jolly Roger, 109
Joseph, Chief, 55–57
Justin Morgan, 47, 117, 123–25

K
Kentucky Saddler, 32
Kiger Mustang, 143–45
Knabstrupper, 61

L
LaCroix, Gene, 147
Lakin, Harry, 3

The Lark Ascending, 27
Lee, Robert E., 43
Leon, Ponce de, 95
Leopard, 89
Linden Tree, 89
Lippizzan, 53
Little Sorrel, 43
Littleton, Rick, 144
Lokai, 73, 76
Look Who's Larkin', 27
Lusitano, 67, 68
Lyons, John, 61

M

Martin, Sunny, 76
Max #2, 90, 92
McCutcheon, Ralph, 43
Merry Walker, 199
Mesohippus, ix
Messenger, 184–85
Miniature Horse, 100, 101–7
    breed characteristics, 102, 103–7,
        105, 107
    breed history, 101–2
    comparable breed, 103
    famous horses, 107
Miohippus, ix
Missouri Fox Trotter, 108, 109–15
    breed description, 111, 112–14,
        114–15
    breed history, 109–11, 110
    comparable breed, 115
    famous horses, 115
Missouri Fox Trotting Horse Breed
    Association, 111, 202
Misty, 87
Misty II, 87
Misty of Chincoteague (Henry), 79, 84
Montana, Joe, 28
Morab, 116, 117–21
    breed characteristics, 118, 119–21,
        120

breed history, 117–19
comparable breeds, 119
Morgan, 122, 123–32
    breed characteristics, 126–28,
        129–32, 130, 133
    breed history, 123–25, 124,
        128–29
    comparable breed, 129
    famous horses, 132
    and Morab, 117, 119
Morgan, Justin, 124–25
Morgan Horse Club, 128
Mr. Ed, 43, 159
Mustang, 134, 135–45
    adopting a, 141–43
    breed characteristics, 143, 144
    breed history, 135–37, 136,
        138–40, 141
    and Chincoteague Pony, 81
    comparable breed, 142
    famous horses, 145
    Kiger Mustang, 143–45
Mustang Lady, 145

N

Napoleon, 50
Narragansett Pacer, 31–32
    and Standardbred, 183
National Cutting Horse Association
    (NCHA), 16
National Horse Show, 34, 35
National Reining Horse Association
    (NHRA), 16
National Show Horse, 146,
    147–54
    breed characteristics, 149, 150,
        151–54, 153, 155
    breed history, 147–48, 148
    comparable breed, 152
    famous horses, 154
National Show Horse Registry,
    147–48, 151, 152, 154, 204

Native Americans, horses of
  American Paint, 10
  Appaloosa, 53, 55–57
  Bashkir Curly, 74
  Chickasaw Pony, 20
Nautical, 159
Navicular disease, 26
Nevada Joe Sterling, 145
New Forest Pony, 84
Nez Percé, and Appaloosa, 55–57
North American Morab Association,
  119

O

Oak Hill Chief, 35
Old Granny, 3
Old King, 45, 46–47
Old Skip, 109, 115
Old Tobe, 176, 181
Orlov Trotter, 195
Overo. *See* American Paint Horse

P

Pace, 180, 185
Palm, Lynn, 27
Palomino, 156, 157–63
  breed characteristics, 158, 159,
    160–62
  breed history, 157, 159
  famous horses, 159
Parelli, Pat, 145
Paso Fino, 95, 115
Patchen Beauty, 50–51
Patches #1, 90, 92
Peruvian Paso, 95, 98
Phantom Wings, 87
Pintos. *See also* American Paint,
  9–10
Plain Justin Bar, 29
Plantation Walker. *See* Tennessee
  Walking Horse

Pliohippus, ix–x
Pony Express, and Morgans, 125
Pony of the Americas, 164, 165–69
  breed characteristics, 168
  breed history, 165–67, 166
  and children, 168, 169, 169
  comparable breed, 167
Pony Penning Days, 80–81, 82, 83,
  84–85
Pushoverture, 173

Q

Quarter boots, 40
Quarter Running Horse, 10

R

Racing, breeds for
  American Quarter Horse, 20–22, 21
  Appaloosa, 60
  Bashkir Curly, 75–76
  Missouri Fox Trotter, 109
  Morab, 121
  Morgan, 124–25
  Standardbred, 183, 184
Rack, 38, 172
Racking Horse, 170, 171–73
  breed characteristics, 172–73, 173
  breed history, 171–72
  famous horses, 173
Rain, 17
Rakush, 53
Rambling Willie, 189
Rangerbred. *See* Colorado Ranger Horse
Read, Thomas Buchanan, 132
Redford, Robert, 29
Rex McDonald, 35
Rienzi, 132
Rierson, C. T., 3–4
Rocky Mountain Horse, 174, 175–81
  breed characteristics, 177, 178, 179,
    180–81

breed history, 176–78
comparable breed, 180
Old Tobe, 181
Rocky Mountain Horse Association
    (RMHA), 176–77, 203
Rodgers Perfection, 199
Rogers, Roy, 159, 199
Rose Parade, breeds in
    American Cream Draft Horse, 7
    American Saddlebred, 43
    Bashkir Curly, 76
Ruby, Mike, 90
Rugged Lark, 27
Running walk, 192, 193, 194
Russian Lokai, 73, 76

S

"Saddle gaits," 34–35
Screw worm, 97
Shatner, William, 43
Sheridan, Philip, 132
Sheridan's Ride (Read), 132
Shetland Pony, 101, 103
    and Pony of the Americas, 165–66
Show jumping, Appaloosa, 59
Show walk, 181
Silver, 50, 199
Silver Lace, 3
Slow gait, 38
Soring, 172, 196–97
Sorraia, 95
South American Criollo, 67, 95, 103
Spanish horses, 9–10
    and American Quarter Horse, 20
    and Azteca, 65–68
    and Florida Cracker Horse, 95
    and Kiger Mustang, 143–44
    and Palomino, 157, 159
    and Rocky Mountain Horse, 178
Spanish Mustang, 95
Sparlock, 76
Spartacus, 77

Speed. *See* Racing, breeds for
Spirit: Stallion of the Cimarron, 17
Standardbred, 182, 183–89
    breed characteristics, 185, 186,
        187–88, 188
    breed history, 183–85
    comparable breed, 189
    famous horses, 188–89
    and Missouri Fox Trotter, 110
    and Morgan, 129
Standardbred Pleasure Horse
    Organization, 187, 204
Steens Mountain Kiger Registry, 144
Stormy, 87
Stormy, Misty's Foal, 87
Strolling Jim, 199
Sultan's Great Day, 43
Sundust, 199
"Switches," 39–40

T

Tail setting, American Saddlebred, 38,
    39–40
Tennessee Walking Horse, 190,
    191–99
    breed characteristics, 192, 194,
        194–96, 197, 198
    breed history, 191–92, 193
    comparable breed, 195
    famous horses, 199
    and Missouri Fox Trotter, 110
    and Morgan, 129
    and Racking Horse, 171–72
    and soring, 196–97
Tennessee Walking Horse Breeder's and
    Exhibitors Association (TWHBEA),
    196–97, 204
Tennessee Walking Horse Breeder's
    Association of America, 192
Thompson, Caleb, 45, 47–48
Thompson, Claude, 57
Thompson, Hudson, 45, 47

Thoroughbred. *See* English
    Thoroughbred
Tinker Horse, 13
Tobiano. *See* American Paint Horse
Tolt, 180
Tovero. *See* American Paint Horse
Traveler, 43
Trigger, 159
Trigger Junior, 199
Trot, 184, 185
    fox, 110, 114
    park, 38
    posting, 191
True Briton, 123
Tuttle, Sam, 176

U
USA Equestrian (USAEq), 16

V
"Varnish," Appaloosa pattern, 58

W
Wahoo King, 17
Wap Spotted, 63
Welsh Pony, 167
West, settlement of
    and American Saddlebred, 32
    and Mustang, 135–37
    and Quarter Horse, 22
Whipple, A. C., 89–90
White Beauty, 50
The White Fox, 51
White Horse Troupe, 47
Wild Free-Roaming Horse and Burro
    act, 137, 138
Wimpy, 23
Winchester, 132
Wing Commander, 35
Wisp o' Mist, 87

Y
Yancy No. 3, 3
Yellow Mount, 17